THE
COMPUTER

IN THE
UNITED STATES

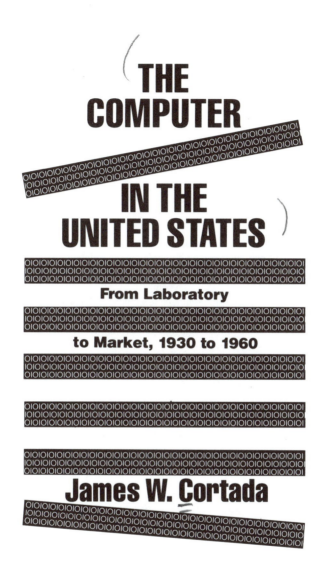

THE COMPUTER

IN THE UNITED STATES

From Laboratory

to Market, 1930 to 1960

James W. Cortada

M.E. Sharpe
Armonk, New York
London, England

Library of Congress Cataloging-in-Publication Data

Cortada, James W.
The computer in the United States : from laboratory
to market, 1930–1960 / James Cortada.
p. cm.
Includes bibliographical references and index.
ISBN 1-56324-234-6.
ISBN 1-56324-235-4 (pbk.)
1. Computer engineering—United States—History.
2. Computers—United States—History.
3. Computer industry—United States—History.
I. Title.
TK7885.A5C67 1993
338.4′70040973—dc20
93-4184
CIP

Printed in the United States of America
The paper used in this publication meets the minimum
requirements of American National Standard for
Information Sciences—Permanence of Paper for
Printed Library Materials, ANSIZ 39.48-1984.

♾

MV (c) 10 9 8 7 6 5 4 3 2 1
MV (p) 10 9 8 7 6 5 4 3 2 1

To James N. Cortada and Shirley B. Cortada

Contents

Illustrations

Tables and Figures

Acronyms

ABC	Atanosoff-Berry Computer
ACE	Automatic Computing Engine
ACM	Association for Computing Machinery
AEC	Atomic Energy Commission
AIEE	American Institute of Electrical Engineers
ALGOL	ALGOLrithmic Language
AMA	American Management Association
ASCC	Automatic Sequence Controlled Calculator
AT&T	American Telephone and Telegraph
BINAC	Binary Automatic Computer
BIZMAC	an RCA computer
BRL	Ballistics Research Laboratory
CAD/CAM	computer-aided design/computer-aided manufacturing
CDC	Control Data Corporation
CEC	Consolidated Electrodynamics Corporation
CIO	Congress of Industrial Organizations
CPC	Card Programmed Calculator
CRC	Computer Research Corporation
DB	data base
EDP	electronic data processing
EDSAC	Electronic Delay Storage Automatic Calculator
EDVAC	Electronic Discrete Variable Automatic Computer
ENIAC	Electronic Numerical Integrator and Computer
ERA	Engineering Research Associates
FORTRAN	FORmula TRANslator
GNP	gross national product
IAS	Institute for Advanced Study

IBM	International Business Machines
IRE	Institute of Radio Engineers
LISP	LISt Processing
MIT	Massachusetts Institute of Technology
NBS	National Bureau of Standards
NCR	National Cash Register
NDRC	National Defense Research Committee
NPL	National Physical Laboratory
RAMAC	Random Access Method of Accounting and Control
R&D	research and development
SAGE	Semiautomatic Ground Environment
SCP	System Control Program
SEA	Société d'Electronique et d'Automatisme
SEAC	U.S. Bureau of Standards Eastern Automatic Computer
SHOT	Society of Historians of Technology
SMS	Standard Modular System
SSEC	Selective Sequence Electronic Calculator
STRETCH	project that developed the IBM 7030
SWAC	U.S. Bureau of Standards Western Automatic Computer
UNIVAC	Universal Automatic Computer

Preface

To the industrialized world the computer is easily an icon of late-twentieth-century society. One increasingly sees acceptance of the notion that the computer is affecting profoundly the structure of economies, jobs, and organizations. The information-processing industry it fomented now hovers at $1 trillion when one adds up the costs of hardware, services, and professional salaries. But computers are simply one product of many new technologies in the past two hundred years, including telephones, automobiles, airplanes, atomic weapons, and television. As a result, historians, economists, sociologists, and philosophers have spent an enormous amount of energy studying the development and use of technology.

The literature on the subject is vast and growing.[1] The history of technology alone is a recognized subfield complete with its own society (Society of Historians of Technology [SHOT]), annual conventions, and journal (*Technology and Culture*). Historians have taken to heart the necessity to explain the increase in technology use over centuries, often arguing that this recent phenomenon is simply an extension of a process long under way. But now their work seems more compelling, more central to understanding how modern society functions.[2]

How does a technological innovation emerge from the creator's mind and enter a society's economy? Many ancillary questions also are raised. Who creates the technology? How does technology work itself into the economy in the first place? How much can a society absorb? How does the public hear about it? How long does the process take? When is a particular technological innovation superseded by others? These are very important questions. Some historians have generalized about these processes, whereas others have chosen to look at specific examples, such as electricity, telecommunications, the telephone, the automobile, electricity, and television.[3] All these efforts are very instructive and contribute to a growing awareness of the process by which a complex technology surfaces in society today. They also emphasize that, once again, researchers lack consensus on the subject.

The case of the computer is instructive. Historians have begun to study the evolution of the computer, have documented how specific machines were built, have begun writing histories of the vendors who market these engines, and have only just begun to study how they have been used.[4] A great deal of research is under way on the history of computing.

In this work I first summarize briefly what is known today about the early history of this technology. I then introduce the general public and those interested in the history of technology at large to the ways by which computers entered the economy and were accepted. First, I review how computer technology was created. Even for the specialist, some of the detail is new as is most of the bibliography upon which it is based. Second, I describe how potential vendors who ultimately sold the machine first reacted to this technology. This is an important exercise because no complex technology enters the economy today without being manufactured and sold by a company. Third, I examine how the American public came to hear about the computer in the first decade of its commercial existence (1950s). I contend, of course, that customers will not acquire what they do not know about.

This book, therefore, is a case study of how one technology evolved from laboratory to market and then went to customers. I identify a relatively distinct three-phase process: creation of the technology, adoption by manufacturers, and acceptance by the public. The second and third phases occurred simultaneously, whereas the first continued beyond its initial thrust in response to activities taking place during the second and third phases. The case of the computer is very instructive for the study of all complex technologies in modern society.

I have limited this case study to the very earliest period of the computer, from the 1930s, when it was under development, through the late 1950s, when it finally achieved commercial success. I ignored the period from the late 1950s to the present because it is less instructive about how a technology first appears. The material I present is not a definitive history of the period or of the technology; it is selective to elucidate the process at work.

   This particular study grew out of an earlier work on the history of the office appliance industry in the United States from 1865 to 1956.[5] In both instances I focus primarily on the American experience of developers, vendors, and customers. In the office appliance industry many technologies have been developed, introduced to the public, and ultimately adopted, including the typewriter, the cash register, adding and calculating machines, punched-card tabulating equipment, and, finally, the computer. Both the office appliance and the computer industries achieved their important form and greatest penetration in the United States economy. The office appliance industry adopted and came to dominate the computer as an extension of its existing product set and sold it to the same customers.

   In chapter 1 I introduce some concepts familiar to specialists in technological innovations and introductions and the questions such products are facing in the 1990s. In chapters 2 and 3 I narrate the history of the technical development of the computer. In chapter 4 I concentrate on how vendors responded to the creation of the computer and came to add it to their product lines. In chapter 5 I review how the American public and, consequently, users of such technology first learned of it during the 1940s and 1950s. In chapter 6 I draw together some lessons and compare the experience of the computer with those of earlier office appliance technologies. In the bibliographic essay I highlight publications that influenced this monograph and can lead the reader to more details on basic themes.

   Sources upon which I based the book, however, are more fully documented in the notes. Most of the sources are contemporary published materials, especially articles and conference papers, and some archival material from the Burroughs Papers at the Charles Babbage Institute. The body of contemporary material on the subject is vast, far more so than previous studies of the computer would indicate, and, therefore, I have carefully introduced this material in context.

   I have included a number of tables as sources of data for those who wish to continue to study this technology and the larger theme. Illustrations make many of the described events less abstract and suggest how appearances and frequency of images portrayed helped establish a concept of computers in the minds of those who would eventually use these machines.

   This book is devoid of elegant paradigms or complex theoretical constructs because historians simply do not know enough about this technology to presume a fixed answer to the question of how technologies are created, introduced to, and accepted by the public. Although trained as an historian, I am first and foremost a business man who has lived in the computer industry for two decades. I have sold, used, and brought to market computer products. Perched as I have been at IBM, I have had a relatively comprehensive view of the currents affecting the information systems industry. Historians have scarcely scratched the surface in understanding this industry. Economists have been too single-issue focused, and social historians have almost ignored the subject. I do not pretend that this book is definitive. It is a warning, however, that the subject of technology transfer from laboratory to market is a very complicated story.

Acknowledgments

I owe an enormous debt of gratitude to many people who helped in special ways as this book grew from concept to published form. The text benefited from a very early reading of several chapters by William Aspray, director of the Center for the History of Electrical Engineering at the Institute of Electrical Electronics Engineers. Alan Stone, of the University of Houston, played an equally important role in advising how best to improve the text. Bruce Bruemmer, of the Charles Babbage Institute at the University of Minnesota, once again helped find illustrations. I am also deeply grateful to David K. Allison, at the National Museum of American History, for finding contemporary portrait photographs of John Mauchly and J. Presper Eckert—a real coup. A particular debt of gratitude must be acknowledged to John Maloney, manager of the IBM Archives, because he was always responsive, supplied me with most of the illustrations for this book, and worked quickly with a positive attitude. I am grateful to Michael Weber, executive editor at M. E. Sharpe, for showing faith in this project. Finally, I owe a special thanks to Virginia M. Barker for once again taking on the daunting task of copyediting one of my books.

THE
COMPUTER

IN THE
UNITED STATES

1

Issues and the Debate

How technology is created, injected into an economy, and, finally, accepted as part of a society's "bag of tools" is an important issue because it is central to understanding the dynamics of creating and using technology. Those who most debate the issue—historians—have only recently begun to wrestle with the question. For many decades they focused on the history of individual devices or classes of technology and machines and have paid little attention to broader concepts of how technology in general emerges or is used.[1] Since the late 1970s, in almost every niche of technology's history, the debate has broadened in two directions: conceptualizing a paradigm that describes the evolution of technology and placing technological events in broad contexts. Those interested in defining such a model follow in the footsteps of science historians who have long studied how scientific change occurs and have often focused on the dramatic by using the word *revolution* to characterize great change.[2] The second effort has placed technological events in a broader societal context rather than dealing with issues as discrete, isolated topics. Thus, instead of histories of clock mechanics or the evolution of printing, one now finds solid work on the effects of clocks[3] or printing[4] on society.

Historians tend to study specific technologies before examining them in a broader context. Thus, it was natural that they would work on the history of steam engines, railroads, weapons, farm implements, and tools such as hammers and knives, and modern airplanes, automobiles, radios, movies, telephones, typewriters, and rockets, to mention only an obvious few.[5] Computers did not escape similar treatment. Most of the major devices from the ENIAC of the 1940s up to and including the International Business Machines personal computer (IBM PC) of the 1980s have been studied by historians, journalists, and engineers. In fact, the majority of the technical histories of the computer business center around descriptions of machines and how they came into being.[6]

Frontiers between the history of science, technology, and, most recently, business have begun to blur, suggesting that those who study the technology of the nineteenth and twentieth centuries will have to acknowledge the interaction of all three. For example, work begun in the 1800s advanced the study of electricity and the effect it had on specific components and elements. These scientific insights were applied to the development of electronic components, such as wire and the light bulb, and, eventually, the radio, early examples of the interdependence of scientific research and technological application.

By the early 1900s applied technology developed products that could be sold. By the 1920s electrical appliances for the home were common. In the 1930s and 1940s researchers in commercial laboratories studied the electrical properties of substances such as silicon and germanium (Bell Laboratories). That study eventually resulted in creation of the transistor in the 1940s and its application in high-speed general-purpose computers by the late 1950s. But converting, for example, scientific understanding of how electricity influences the properties of silicon into a product that could be sold (e.g., an IBM computer) was the work of businesses although such projects were often funded by U.S. government agencies. Remington Rand, IBM, and other computer vendors of the 1950s and 1960s would not have gone through the effort of applying this technology unless they had had some expectation that the government or society would accept the equipment by renting and buying it.

The interrelationship among science, technology, and business becomes increasingly obvious in Europe and in North America as one moves through the nineteenth century. Charles Headrick, in a series of books, has elucidated clearly the process of technology's development and export in the nineteenth century. When reading his books, one also sees a good example of how technology's history can be examined in the broader context of a society's activities. In his telecommunications example he shows the effects of that technology on diplomacy and imperialism in the nineteenth century.[7]

Examples from the twentieth century far outnumber those for the nineteenth because so many technologies came to the fore, almost always the results of work done in organizations: government laboratories, corporate research and development (R&D) facilities, and universities. Thus, all three types of organizations worked together to develop the most important technologies of this period.[8] The most dramatic example of how technology emerges is the computer; in chapters 2 and 3, I discuss the development of this device as a by-product of interdependent work in those three types of institutions. The debate about how technology evolved in the modern period has shifted over time. In the 1950s and 1960s, for example, viewing technology as applied science was a widely supported approach. Scientists discovered principles, and technologists applied them. According to that logic, then, businesses sold products on the basis of the technology they offered. Edwin Layton and others in the 1970s suggested the paradigm that now dominates historians' thinking on the issue. Layton argued that science and technology were two separate fields but that they interacted. Each had its own methods, values, and history.[9] By the beginning of the 1990s the call went out to perceive the two as more intertwined. Eda Kranakis argued that a more realistic approach was to view the interaction dynamics of science and technology as from fields that overlapped "intermeshing realms of social activity."[10] In fact, this call for a new view reflected a process already under way during the 1970s and 1980s.[11]

The debate over the nature of scientific and technological history is also animated by concerns about the philosophies or attitudes of technology's historians[12] and, more esoterically, the role of determinism and indeterminacy in technology's history.[13] In the 1970s and 1980s historians began to deal with the more practical issue of acceptance of technology as part of the debate.

Because acceptance of technology is an issue crucial to understanding the success of the computer, it is important to appreciate how innovations are received. Understanding greatly influences the speed of adoptions, nature of changes made, and effects of social policy. Historians are beginning to understand that new technologies were not automatically accepted when they were introduced. In an earlier monograph I argue that the typewriter was not widely accepted at first. Store clerks resisted using the cash register, and Herman Hollerith spent years developing his punched-card business.[14] Daniel Headrick shows that the American military community often resisted adoption of new innovations in the nineteenth century.[15] David F. Noble shows that computer-aided design and manufacturing (CAD/CAM) uses of the computer to design aircraft in the 1950s and 1960s were adopted less for the direct economic benefits or productivity they offered than because the United States Air Force insisted that they be used by military suppliers.[16] Headrick hit upon one of the more important reasons why a technology is not always immediately accepted: "Innovations bring about changes in power and procedures and threaten old traditions; worse yet, changes favor the young and rebellious."[17] Headrick argues that innovations then only come when forced by competition. James R. Beniger offers a slightly different version. He, too, recognizes that innovations were accepted only with reason. Citing the modern American economy of the late 1800s and early 1900s, he argues that new technologies in office appliances were adopted to regain control over productive means within the economy. He shows a correlation between when the crisis of control first emerged (post–Civil War period) and the simultaneous development of various communication technologies (e.g., telephone, typewriter, and punched-card equipment) to fix the problem.[18]

Business historians have frequently dealt with the effects of technology on companies and industries. They acknowledge the profound effects technologies have on company development and evolution. Without technology, for example, would DuPont have become the chemical and pharmaceutical giant that it did?[19] What about IBM?[20] For more than thirty years Alfred Chandler has studied the nature of corporate structures in American society and has demonstrated that large corporations in part became possible as technological innovations in manufacture, transportation, and communications allowed a new class of workers (managers) to emerge capable of coordinating the activities of thousands of employees across whole continents. Railroad companies were Chandler's favorite examples of the interaction between technology and business, but he also cited numerous other cases, ranging from sewing machines to chemical companies.[21] Railroads represented an excellent example of nineteenth-century technology to study, and the computer serves a similar purpose for the twentieth century.

In a broad-based study of industrial development in Western Europe from the mid eighteenth century forward, David S. Landes suggests how science, technology, economics, business, and society interrelate and affect each other. More than an economic history of Europe, *The Unbound Prometheus* is a model of how all the issues mentioned can be pieced together. Because the history of the computer will ultimately have to be placed in such a broad context, owing to its recognized pervasive presence in late-twentieth-century societies, Landes may point to a way to do so.

He explains that economic history can be viewed as a race for wealth and that this race sped up during the nineteenth and twentieth centuries. The race quickened partly because the ability to apply technology faster reached the point where "man can now order technological and scientific advance as one orders a commodity."[22] Modernization of Europe's economy, which began in the late 1800s, came, in part, from the growth of scientific branches of manufacture. Landes places particular emphasis on the role of social and cultural factors, such as the attitudes and positions of engineers in Germany, who practice their trade as they were taught. He also notes that each society combines a variety of factors, traditions, possibilities, circumstances, wealth, and materials to formulate a response to economic development. Among the critical historical forces at work are the abilities of institutions to respond to change and change itself. Thus, the speed with which engineers can accumulate information, apply it, and present products affects the level of technological innovations in a country. One sees that process at work in the computer industry in the United States.[23]

Such an expansive view calls forth some obvious questions that should be asked when examining how technologies emerge and are applied in a particular society. How are science and technology organized in a society? How do they come together to achieve results? How do organized science, technology, and business function? To what extent does the experience of the computer industry elucidate answers to these questions? Finally, what effect does a particular technology have on society's view of the world? Will the computer, to select a specific example, change society's perspective of the world and its philosophy as did the discoveries of earlier people, such as navigators in the fifteenth century or builders of mechanical devices in the Middle Ages? D. S. L. Cardwell in his study, *Turning Points in Western Technology*, implies that the answer will be yes.[24]

In an attempt to bring together into one explanation the evolution of technology, with suggested points of reference for the kinds of questions raised here, George Basalla proposed that one look at three themes: diversity, which suggests that many kinds of things exist; necessity, which assumes that people invent what they need to take care of their basic needs; and technological evolution, which he defines as an organic analogy in that things evolve over time and are chosen for reasons similar to those that cause animals to evolve one way instead of another.[25] He argues that a basic rule is at work in the evolution of technology, namely, that "any new thing that appears in the made world is based on some object already in existence."[26] He cites the example of the transistor's development as a case in point: "Because the transistor was perceived as a replacement for a triode in a circuit, and because vacuum tube manufacturers turned to transistor production, features peculiar to thermionic tubes were transferred to the transistor."[27]

His rule also applies to the development of the computer. He observes that things change in form and application from their original designs to accommodate changes demanded by society. Automobile designs are modified to meet stylistic or pollution control regulations, for example. Clearly, during the information-handling hardware evolution in the 1920s and 1930s, users knowledgeable about such equipment demanded additional capacity and function that would only have made sense once they had used and appreciated existing machines.[28] Basalla also points out, as did Landes, that different societies encourage unique changes to basic knowledge.[29]

Basalla reflects the thinking of many historians of the post-1970 period in that he, too, recognizes an interchange of ideas back and forth between scientists and engineers. The case of the computer confirms that practice. In his highly influential book, *Invention and Economic Growth,* Jacob Schmookler postulates that inventors took preexisting technology and scientific knowledge "off the shelf" and put it together to develop new devices.[30] He places heavy emphasis on market demand for such an approach, and, at first blush, the argument seems confirmed by Beniger, who saw that the need for control over processes (market demand) caused inventors to develop information-handling equipment. The single causal effect approach to the study of technology's evolution, however, flies in the face of reality and remains increasingly unsupported as historians find causality to result from a number of factors: social, cultural, scientific, technological, and economic.

Thus, all of these arguments, preferences of theory, and observations of events lead the student of the evolution of technology to focus on a larger set of questions than before. These questions concern the interplay of science and technology, the role of antecedent devices or technologies, the needs of society, economic and cultural incentives, the influence of individuals (inventors and corporate executives), and the role of corporations, university laboratories, and government agencies.

In the case of the computer, one sees the entire galaxy of elements at work. First, scientists worked on aspects of physics that later influenced the invention and construction of computers. Second, the existence of university laboratories, especially those at the Massachusetts Institute of Technology (MIT), provided a channel for focused scientific and engineering activity that led directly to the creation of the computer. Third, the extent of funding and general support provided by the U.S. government was crucial and unique to computer development in the United States. Fourth, it would be difficult to imagine the success of the computer in the 1950s and 1960s without its adoption as a product line by office appliance vendors, some of whom had existed since the 1880s. Electrical manufacturers looked at the computer but failed to deliver it to market effectively; office appliance vendors became the primary delivery vehicle for such technology. Finally, the nature of American interest in scientific and technological innovation in a society that had information delivery vehicles, such as a free press, nationally distributed magazines, and technical and business journals, made it possible to educate and inform a public that ultimately would have to fund the development, manufacture, and use of the computer.

In short, it was no accident that the computer experienced its greatest development in the United States, even though very important work on its creation also occurred in Great Britain, and, to a lesser extent, elsewhere in Europe. It was also no accident that its acceptance would be greatest first in the United States where, in particular, government support in the early phases of computer development reduced economic risks for suppliers. Although the story of its successful implementation is outside the scope of this book, more computers were installed sooner in the United States than anywhere else in the world, and most of the innovations of the 1950s through the 1980s originated in the United States. The circumstances that made that position possible were already in place in the 1930s to 1950s.[31]

By looking at three aspects of the computer's development, distribution, and awareness in its early history, one can test many of the ideas and challenges posed by economists and historians and cited here. One can also go back to other technological introductions and apply a similar narrative approach, investigating the interrelationship of all three issues. This approach allows historians to summarize early experience with one of the most important technological introductions of the twentieth century.

I offer the following model. Principles of science, identified primarily in universities, were applied to the development of computing devices that evolved primarily from office appliances in the 1920s and 1930s. These efforts were funded usually by U.S. government contracts applied first to scientific and engineering uses. By the early 1940s two lines of development were clearly evident—analog and digital computing. By the late 1940s government-supported research (by now evident in university laboratories, government agencies, and private firms) also led to creation of new components (such as diodes and transistors) that, during the 1950s, enhanced the technical capabilities of these machines. In chapters 2 and 3 I describe this process at work.

The next phase of technology transfer from laboratory to market applied the machine to uses in government, science, and engineering, then to business or commercial requirements (such as accounting, production, and inventory control). That process of migration from laboratory to subsidized government/scientific users to business markets occurred essentially from the 1940s to the early 1950s; it is the subject of chapter 4.

As computer technology migrated out of laboratories into recognizable devices, it was introduced to potential buyers and users and to the public at large, the subject of chapter 5. I review both the literature and the American buying process to suggest what happened. Although this examination of the subject is not definitive, it clearly shows that both customers and the public were introduced to the machine at the same time. This literature—different for the public than for the potential customer—reinforced each one's image of the computer's potential benefits. That positive view led to a set of uses expanded from specific military and scientific applications to those for business. With that broadening of use, the computer had arrived as a commercially viable product. By the early 1960s, business applications far outnumbered military and scientific uses. Commercial acceptance made possible the growth of the data-processing industry to the point where today it comprises about 5 percent of the U.S. gross national product (GNP).

Nothing happens in isolation. Despite the unique qualities of computer technology (e.g., extensive U.S. government support), its arrival paralleled to a considerable extent the emergence of office equipment technologies in the late nineteenth and early twentieth centuries. By comparing and contrasting these events in chapter 6, I link the arrival of the computer to the broader historical process of technology's general evolution and, more specifically, to the long history of the human search for aids to handle information.

2

Technical Origins of the Computer

The information-processing industry is "high tech" because its products and services rely on sophisticated technologies that grew out of advanced studies in physics, biology, mechanical engineering, chemistry, electricity, and improved manufacturing techniques. Continued success in this industry has always depended on a steady flow of improvements in performance, reliability, capacity, and declining prices (from the late 1940s to the present). The significant expansion of scientific discoveries in the nineteenth century that I. Bernard Cohen identified as a scientific revolution,[1] coupled with research and development activities in the twentieth century, facilitated the rapid application of new knowledge to the creation of the computer industry. The development and use of the computer is a complex evolution of an existing industry (office appliance) that migrated from reliance on mechanical devices for handling information to electronically based machines (1920s to 1940s), which themselves, in time, were replaced by computers (late 1950s to 1960s) capable of more function per unit cost. It is a story of scientific discoveries and technological advances coming together and being eventually adopted by the office appliance industry. Adoptions frequently occurred in the formative stages with significant U.S. government support. The modern data-processing industry finally emerged in the late twentieth century.

No technological advance seems to have drawn as much attention as the computer. Writers about modern technology have been very eager to describe its origins.[2] They are quick to point out how one particular machine or another was built. They describe its role almost as if it were a worn-out tale. The literature on general computer history has increased enormously.[3] Most of these works emphasize the technological evolution of various machines. Some, in the 1980s, began to acknowledge economic or industrial factors that contribute to computer development.[4] Most writers on the subject are scientists and engineers (often with direct experience building the machines they write about), journalists, and economists; a few are practicing historians.[5] As a result, the history of the computer is frequently told in simplistic terms, often with cause and effect stated too glibly or too narrowly, and without placing its development into the context of economic and political history. In these accounts, demand and use are almost always minor concerns, when, in fact, without these elements there would have been no requirement to have computers.

Overview of Motives and Origins

The truth about the evolution of computers includes a combination of causes that made creation of the computer possible and, more importantly, led to its effective use as a replacement for older devices and manual methods for handling information. Without the latter two developments and influences, the computer would simply not have been sufficiently important to justify serious historical examination. Computers would have been relegated to the curious, as most computational equipment constructed before the 1870s had been. One has only to recall the lack of significant interest in calculating machines in the seventeenth and eighteenth centuries to realize that a technology becomes important historically not when it is developed but when it is applied in a practical and cost-effective manner.

One can summarize the development of the computer into a practical tool that economically supported an industry by looking at several clusters of reasons, some of which were more important at one time than another but all of which were operative all the time. First, science had to evolve to lay the basis for development as it had for the study of electricity in the nineteenth century. As late as the 1930s, development required Alan Turing's initial work on information theory. Second, the application of new scientific knowledge to solve problems, for example, for the military and scientific communities, was needed. Engineers, scientists, and mathematicians adopted the new technology when they applied scientific knowledge to construct new workable devices. When these machines became more competitive in cost, function, and reliability than other information-handling devices, they perceived such equipment as supporting a new line of business. Buried in both scientific and technological changes were others in materials and manufacturing topics awaiting their historians. If, for example, vacuum tubes had not become available in the early 1900s along with more reliable manufacturing methods by the late 1930s, the earliest computers would not have been built in the 1930s and early 1940s. Manufacturers recognized that new materials and advanced ways to package components and fabricate machines could drive down manufacturing costs. Productivity could also be enhanced by new production processes that used better tools and, subsequently, by electronics, chemistry, and, in the late 1970s, by lithography and other advanced methods. IBM, for one, paid enormous attention to manufacturing methods throughout its long history in an attempt to lower equipment costs. That principle was applied just as intensively to computers, which, before 1950, had been built one by one much like designer jewelry.[6]

Individuals alone could not bring the computer to reality or to market. Devices designed by Charles Babbage in the early 1800s, Percy E. Ludgate in the first years of the twentieth century, and Leonardo Torres y Quevedo in the 1910s and 1920s, among others, were not computers. The earliest machines that could possibly claim such a name—for example, the Colossus, ENIAC, Harvard Mark I, or the IAS machine—required the coordination of many types of skills. The electrician had to work with the engineer and the mathematician with the physicist to make it happen. That kind of combined effort required teams of workers, which called for process management. That requirement was best satisfied by institutions where these individuals worked, such as MIT, Harvard University, and the University of Pennsylvania's Moore School of Electrical Engineering. Budgets for such projects were large, and their support came more from the U.S. government than from any other single source throughout the 1930s, 1940s, and 1950s (see chapter 3). When specific applications were perceived as advantageous (profitable and economically low-risk investments), companies helped. For example, work on network analyzers at MIT between World Wars I and II received financial help from utility companies. American Telephone and Telegraph (AT&T) sought better switching mechanisms for telephone calls and, thus, supported analog research at Bell Labs in the 1920s and 1930s. For these reasons the story of the computer was not limited to one scientific or technological development or series of inventions but included the reality of institutional support for leadership, facilities, and budgets. These components helped the embryonic computer stand on its own economically by responding to commercial customer demand.[7]

Given the scientific and technological advances and institutional support that came, the absolute necessity for the creation of computing was the establishment or emergence of need for such equipment. Clearly, the history of the office appliance industry shows that demand drove changes in technologies and provided incentives to create new products. Devices were modified and enhanced, and new technologies applied in response to the needs of those who required information-handling equipment. The computer became important once users figured out how to employ these new devices to advantage. They usually looked at function, cost, capability (capacity and speed), reliability, and applications, comparing them to other methods to get work done. This is not to say that the analysis was always done well because misinformation, inexperience, or even the prestige of having such a machine also influenced decisions to acquire them. The period from the late 1940s through the 1950s could just as easily be characterized not as the infancy of the computer but as a time in which its benefits were realized over other alternatives. The lens through which commercial and government users peered at the computer was that of experience with other office appliances. In the 1950s, for example, considerable attention was paid to how computers did things as compared with tabulating and accounting equipment already in use. When the use of computers functionally improved manual applications and decreased costs, such devices were acquired.[8] Nothing was inevitable; the computer was not a historical phenomenon waiting to happen. It was chosen over other alternatives. Thus, prior consumer experience and ability to make choices accompanied the computer on its journey from laboratory to commercial success.

That trip was a long one, realistically, from the 1930s through the 1950s. Although historians gave much attention to the 1950s as the period during which extensive use of computers became possible, their case must not be overstated. The computer had won its place by 1960/61 and, for those who doubt, certainly by 1965. But in 1960–61 only an estimated six thousand computers were operational, a tiny number when compared to how many adding, calculating, and tabulating machines were in use worldwide or when contrasted to the millions of office workers performing tasks that could have been automated.[9] The computer's period of wide acceptance did not begin until the 1960s. By then computers had become more cost effective than older devices and easier and more reliable to use than some manual methods and had sufficient capacity to make the decision to install them sensible.

Another important aspect of computer development was its international character. The Americans and the British cannot realistically claim to be the sole inventors of the computer or of its industry although the Americans, especially, dominated activities. The evolution of scientific knowledge that underlay computer technologies was developed in many countries. The construction of machines and development of theories about them were also the products of work done before World War II in the United States and Great Britain, to a far lesser extent in Germany, France, and Italy, and immediately after the war in the Soviet Union, Japan, and elsewhere. Sometimes developments in various countries appeared almost concurrently (e.g., Zuse and Aiken in the 1930s), whereas other efforts built sequentially on work across international borders (e.g., British and American work on computers in the late 1940s and, especially, on memory systems).

The sale of computers had to be worldwide for many of the same reasons put forth by manufacturers for selling tabulating and accounting equipment across the globe in earlier decades. In time, often, the same suppliers sold computers and office equipment.[10] It was no accident, for example, that Japan became a major computer vendor by the 1970s, or that the Germans and the French had nascent computer industries by the early 1950s.[11]

Acceptance of computers was a story of inventions building on each other, of institutions advancing cautiously in their involvement with such technology, and of users looking back to older methods as a test bed for new ones. Hence, the term *revolutionary* does not make much sense as an adjective to describe the creation and early use of computers. The history of the development of useful computers is better characterized as *evolutionary*, with change over time coming as technologies and applications migrated together down an increasingly more sophisticated path to consumer attraction to such technology. Yet the term *revolution* is embedded in the titles and rhetoric of many books and articles on computer history.[12] Cohen thoughtfully and correctly pointed out that in scientific revolutions, what happens is a fundamental change in the way science is looked at. The computer made possible the alteration of scientific theories "in that logically linked propositions and formal mathematical statements have been replaced by complex computer models."[13]

Economically, the data presented in this volume indicate substantial yet linear improvements in price performance of computers over earlier technologies and among various models from generation to generation of systems. These changes all happened concurrently as demand for computers grew. Therefore, one may speak of the data-processing industry as generally completing its first historical phase in the mid to late 1950s. Up to that time it had been an era essentially without benefit of the computer. One can characterize the data-processing industry (after the mid to late 1950s) as more unified in its dependence on the computer and more advanced technologies embedded in peripheral equipment.

Scientific Preconditions

The technological history of the computer is long and complex. Very clearly, however, a number of independent developments in mathematics and science came together as time passed to make possible the modern computer. Several trends in the evolution of science and mathematics had to merge before the computer could become valuable in these fields. These long lines of evolution predated the computer by generations and specifically included harnessing electricity as a medium for storing, carrying, and manipulating information, on the one hand, and the evolution of mathematics from calculus to Boolean logic, on the other.[14] From these two points came the conceptual designs of information-handling systems that today are called information theory or computer science. The final step was the development of a raft of materials and parts that made possible the actual construction of these engines. All these developments came in a period when circumstances increasingly encouraged their evolution. Thus, the need for practical electricity grew as much out of scientific curiosity as from the growing limits of steam power. When quantitative analysis and the use of statistics became more commonplace in nineteenth-century America and Europe, the need to find better ways to calculate helped generate incentives to develop modern tools.

Electricity, mathematics, physics, and engineering became subjects of intense study during the eighteenth and, particularly, late nineteenth centuries, sometimes parallel to, and on other occasions, in reaction to, developments in other fields. Important advances in understanding these topics were made, beginning in the 1880s. From that decade, extending almost without interruption to World War II, significant developments in each discipline occurred and were known to those working in other fields. Rapid advances made possible the application of newfound knowledge to a variety of uses, which, in turn, encouraged further development of new products and materials. For example, better understanding of electricity partially supported development of the radio, which, in turn, encouraged electrical engineers to study information flow, first through the development of radar but then directly with the digital computer. Boolean mathematics contributed the on/off, positive/negative notion so crucial to the design of the modern computer. Physics and new materials made possible the development of vacuum tubes to store information and, later, the more efficient core memory that finally made it realistic to use the computers known today. Core memories were replaced with silicon chips (integrated circuits) in the 1960s, which evolved in subsequent decades into more efficient, cost-effective forms. In the 1990s, new ceramic materials are appearing that can carry electricity, hence data, with almost no resistance at close to room temperatures, portending enormous increases in capacity with declining costs.

Scientific preconditions evolved as a process in evidence from the mid-nineteenth century to the immediate post–World War I period. In the years between the two world wars, the four lines of development came together so that by World War II one could conceptualize the modern computer and actually build it with known concepts and available materials. Without meeting these basic preconditions, it is difficult to think how engineers could have overcome the challenges of war so quickly, if at all. Because so much development had taken place before the war, scientists and engineers during the conflict witnessed the emergence of electronics as a field of considerable importance with practical experience in data-handling equipment. The years from 1945 to the mid-1950s were characterized as a period during which existing concepts and technologies improved dramatically, making it both cost-effective and functionally realistic to rely on computers to perform tasks and, in the late 1950s, for the office machine industry to support the shift away from mechanical accounting and tabulating equipment. In the rest of this book I document these characteristics at work. Understanding them is important because of the enormous growth in computer use in subsequent decades made possible by volume production and additional refinements to emerging technologies. By then the notion that one could build computers and use them reliably had been established.

The concept of scientific preconditions is useful for appreciating the way in which science, technology, and subsequent acceptance and use of products interplayed to make the evolution of the data-processing industry possible. It causes one to place into broader context the work of individual inventors, government officials, and business leaders. In science the efforts of one individual often build on results communicated by other researchers. This is not to suggest a Newtonian elegance in the process because the chance existed that various decisions and developments would create new circumstances; but, in the final analysis, scientists and business people built on the works of others before them. Executives also worried about the timing of product introductions. (Is it cost-effective enough? Reliable enough? Will anybody buy it?) The experience of data processing and computer science in general demonstrates the process at work.[15]

The idea that developments flow from one point to another in a seemingly uninterrupted stream can also be misleading and, often, too simplistic. Viewed from afar, the evolution of electricity, mathematics, and physics, followed by thousands of developments in applied science, did, in fact, make today's computers what they are. The evolution of computer science, as described in this book, reflects that continuous, almost seamless round of developments. In reality, however, nothing was predictable, and change was not seamless or smooth. Developments were often unpredictable. Cohen caught the spirit of the process when he argued that "an unpredictable revolutionary innovation in one area may provide the means for effecting a revolutionary breakthrough in some other area."[16] The expansion in knowledge of electricity, for example, led by surprise to the development of the transistor, which helped miniaturize electronics in the 1950s and 1960s.[17] In short, the unpredictable actually worked to speed up the development process during the twentieth century in computer science as in other fields.[18]

Electricity

Electricity was known to exist for many centuries, and considerable work was done in the eighteenth century to catalog its features. In 1821 Michael Faraday (1791–1867) applied this knowledge by building one of the first electrical motors. It was an early attempt to harness the perceived power of electricity, and within a generation it had become obvious to scientists and business people that electrical power would be more desirable than steam because it was more reliable and less expensive. By the 1880s electrical light was coming into its own thanks to Thomas A. Edison (1849–1931), the prolific American inventor of such devices as the light bulb (created by many inventors), motion pictures, and the phonograph player. With expansion in the use of electricity came creation of the electrical engineering profession. During the 1880s the methods for creating and harnessing electrical power—as in the chemical industry and, later, in computers—would reveal a pattern of behavior characterized by methodical patent applications, team- and product-oriented applied research, and inventors of electrical components who were more frequently corporate employees than independent operators. It was a process already obvious in the office products industry by World War I.[19]

By the end of the nineteenth century an industry existed to deliver a standard form of electrical power to ever-increasing numbers of customers. During the first four decades of the twentieth century, electrical power became less expensive and more readily available. First, large electrical machines were designed and built, followed by products that, by the end of the 1920s, could be used in the home (e.g., toasters, washing machines, and radios). Throughout these years the use of electrical telephones and light also spread like a grid across the nation.[20] The amount of power consumed made the significance of this new technology to the industrializing world as a whole very obvious (see Table 2.1).

In addition to harnessed electrical power, developments in electrical communications were also prerequisite to the computer. Of the three forms of electrical communications available by World War I—telegraph, telephone, and radio—the latter proved the most important for the early development of the computer. Work on radio transmission in the late 1800s and early 1900s led to the sensationalized success of Guglielmo Marconi (1874–1937). But inadequate components for

Table 2.1

**Electrical Power Production, 1920–40
(billions of kilowatt hours)**

Year	U.S.	Germany	France	Italy	U.K.
1920	30	15	6	5	9
1925	55	20	11	7	12
1930	90	29	17	11	18
1935	98	36	18	14	26
1940	140	62	24	21	38

Sources: David S. Landes, *The Unbound Prometheus* (Cambridge: Cambridge University Press, 1969), 441; Arthur S. Link, *American Epoch: A History of the United States since the 1890's* (New York: Alfred A. Knopf, 1967), 263.

Note: All figures are rounded to whole numbers for convenience and usually represent estimated production data.

transmitting and receiving signals made the radio impractical until Lee De Forest (1873–1961), an American, developed the three-element vacuum tube. That invention, much improved upon in the early decades of the twentieth century, made radio and long-distance telephone communications practical and cost-effective by amplifying incoming signals.

When C-T-R (precursor to IBM) was being put together just before World War I, the first radio companies were also being formed. By the start of the war, AT&T had purchased patent rights to De Forest's vacuum tube, which it went on to improve at Bell Laboratories in the 1920s and 1930s. During World War I the "wireless" radio proved its worth for communications in combat, at sea, and for cryptoanalysis.[21] The telephone played a role too. Its wide acceptance made possible the AT&T Company, whose financial resources supported more research in communications and, later, computers, while creating the demand for computerlike devices during the 1920s and 1930s for use in telephony. These computerlike devices, telephone relays, were used in some calculators in the 1930s and 1940s.

Thus, the demand for electricity and its attendant call for electrified communications had, by the 1930s, created a generation of electrical engineers (many of whom used radios) who came to adulthood perhaps sensing that electrical impulses could carry information rapidly. Many were familiar with the electronic components of the day through hobby and professional use and appreciated their potential applicability in new ways. The same process was at work during the 1970s when other young people interested in electronics and computing, also familiar with components of their day, began to build microcomputers. But in the 1920s, and especially in the 1930s, the realization that electrical impulses could be used to enhance computing by controlling functions was important when combined with technical appreciation of the dynamics of electricity; in effect, these circumstances created the preconditions needed by the early builders of computers.[22]

By the start of World War II electricity had become a well established source of power in the United States and in Europe. It was by then a utility industry some sixty years old. Its scientific features were well appreciated and its applications were extensive and still expanding. The field of electronics (an application of electricity) was just as active. World War II carried the evolution of electricity further; instead of just providing power and electronics, making tools do the muscle work for people, both concepts were applied to calculating. By 1946–47, electronics was seen as the basis for many future significant developments in office equipment and computers.[23]

Mathematics and Information Theory

Mathematical events and the thinking that led to the information theory of the 1950s are essential ancestors of the computer and of the modern data-processing industry. Mathematics and information theory, along with electricity and electronics, came together in the interwar period to make the computer possible. This was most true in the United States but happened concurrently in Western Europe.

For many centuries the idea had existed that thinking and calculations were interrelated. Gottfried Wilhelm Leibniz (1646–1716) repostulated the idea with his universal calculus. He studied characteristics of binary numbers as well. Such combinations of numbers are represented by strings of two symbols; by the late 1800s that notation would be seen as zeroes and ones. Some 150 years after Leibniz worked on the problem George Boole (1815–1864) made the critical leap forward in mathematics that would directly influence the evolution of any computer that used electricity. In his book of 1854, *An Investigation of the Laws of Thought, on Which Are Founded the Mathematical Theories of Logic and Probabilities,* he showed how the principles of "pure" logic could be articulated by employing binary notation of zeroes and ones. With such a system of representation, he could articulate patterns of logic, be they words or numbers. His "Boolean algebra" could express thoughts found in mathematics (relationships of numbers) or in language (non-numeric logical reasoning) using a symbolic language written in algebraic form that also relied on zeroes and ones in various combinations. F. L. G. Frege (1848–1925) applied Boole's theory of sets, and Giuseppe Peano (1858–1932) attempted to reduce arithmetic to the essentials of formal symbolisms in the 1880s. Bertrand A. W. Russell and Alfred North Whitehead published their massive *Principia Mathematica* (1910–13), helping logic become a respected branch of mathematics.[24] To close the link with computers, the notion of binary operations in mathematics corresponded well with the characteristics of electricity in which there was switching of systems (power) on or off shown by Claude Shannon (1916–). One could express that activity just as easily with binary numbers of zeroes and ones with combinations of such numbers representing data. Shannon, among the electrical engineers, was the first to see the relationship clearly, although not until the 1940s.[25]

Shannon, who studied at MIT, and Alan Turing (1912–54) in Great Britain initiated the subsequent round of changes in the 1930s and 1940s that led to the merger of mathematical principles with those of electricity and, then, engineering to create the computer. Neither of these men, however, worked in a vacuum. A very few others were also beginning to pull together the two fields at the same time. In the period bracketing World War I and World War II the idea that the on/off in electricity could be applied to record information was appreciated primarily by engineers at Bell Laboratories.[26] Add the existence of calculators and tabulating gear, and one begins to appreciate the work done to apply machinery to mathematics.

Shannon, more effectively than others, drew the connection between Boolean algebra and electricity during the 1940s at Bell Laboratories. By the time he had developed his view on the subject, Shannon was already aware of work by others in such areas as analog computing (Vannevar Bush was at MIT at the time), network analyzers (at AT&T and MIT since the 1920s), and in development of electronic components.[27] His interest focused on appreciating characteristics of electronic switching circuits made up of electromechanical relays.[28] Relays were either on or off; he wanted to describe their behavior and so turned to Boolean logic, in which a particular state of a relay could be described as either a zero or a one at any time. This process detailed one binary digit (which later became a *bit,* or single character, in computerese) of data. That notion became basic to computer theory. His application of Boolean algebra made it possible for electrical engineers to describe the behavior of electrical systems as a series of binary notations. One could configure an application, that is, articulate what tasks had to be performed, by the combination of zeroes and ones to represent tasks in mathematics or logic.[29]

At the same time that Shannon was being introduced to mathematics and electronics, in Great Britain Alan M. Turing, a brilliant young mathematician, was defining a theoretical process for calculating using a theoretical machine, later known as the Turing Machine. He published a paper in 1937 that is a firm statement of the characteristics of a computational machine.[30] He described a machine that had a tape drive. The tape was partitioned into squares; each square had one of a finite number of symbols or remained blank. The tape could theoretically move in and out of the machine; thereby, the device could scan one square at a time and erase or print symbols. He explained how his machine could perform its functions with just two commands if all problems and commands were expressed in his binary code. In short, he described the steps necessary to accomplish a particular task, which then could be done by a machine. In theory he described a digital computer before it had been built, let alone called that. During World War II Turing was given the opportunity to apply some of his ideas, which he did successfully with the British Colossus computer used to decipher German coded messages.[31]

A further step that refined the notions presented by Turing and Shannon was the work of John Von Neumann (1903–57). He was a giant in twentieth-century mathematics who today is as much remembered for his work in computer science as for that in his own field. By the time World War II arrived, Von Neumann was recognized internationally as an outstanding mathematician. As a consultant to various U.S. government agencies during World War II he was called upon to advise on such practical problems as better methods for calculating ballistics tables and breaking enemy codes. Through his work on the atomic bomb he became familiar with computer projects, which he endorsed. His interest in war-related issues legitimized the study of applied mathematics in an age when mathematicians were more interested in theoretical issues. By 1944 he was corresponding with key developers of computational machines and had become an advisor to the team building the ENIAC, the first functioning electronic digital computer in the United States, built at the Moore School of Electrical Engineering at the University of Pennsylvania.[32]

In addition to calling attention to the value of work being done on computers, Von Neumann made a significant contribution by writing a paper that summarized and refined concepts being developed by John W. Mauchly and others at the Moore School. He crystallized the notion of what the design of a computer should be, describing an architecture that, for all intents and purposes, still defines today's computers. Later known as the Von Neumann Machine, this was a description of the major elements of a computer system and how they interrelated. In perhaps the most famous and influential paper ever written on modern computer science, entitled "First Draft of a Report on EDVAC" (completed in May 1945), Von Neumann laid down the design of a new machine. Initially unpublished, it circulated among the few scientists and engineers working in the United States on various computational projects and influenced their work.[33]

Von Neumann intended his highly theoretical and conceptual paper to describe computers in general and not just the EDVAC (a follow-on to the ENIAC). He said a computer's architecture should consist of five components: arithmetic, central control, memory, input, and output units. Drawing on his background in mathematics, he established a logical structure for his concepts and even went the extra step of drawing analogies to the human central nervous system, reflecting results of some conversations held with Norbert Wiener of MIT in early 1945. These talks may have spurred the emergence of cybernetics—a word Wiener coined to describe the complex "art and science of control" over communications and control in living organisms and machines—as a field when Wiener began publishing on the topic in the late 1940s. Von Neumann, in his paper, described the stored program, a concept that called for all data and instructions to be stored together within one memory system in the computer and managed by the computer. This approach would permit the processor to compute at the speed of electronics while both data and commands were read or written under the control of programs, not peripheral equipment or people. He suggested the reduction and theoretical elimination of human intervention in the performance of tasks, as was then common with IBM and Remington Rand tabulating systems.

The memory unit would store data, which could be either information or instructions, differentiated only when they moved into the processing part of the computer. There they were either data, a program, or instructions that did something to data. He also described how this might be managed with a focus on the logical modification of an instruction or data, using what today would be called either the system control program (SCP) or actual application programs. Von Neumann's document contained a description of the memory, the processor where actual calculations physically occurred, the idea of input/output devices such as printers, card punchers and readers, tape, and other storage media.

By describing how all of these might interact, Von Neumann sharpened what fairly could be called a protoinformation theory as applied to computers and gave focus to computer science, which was not yet recognized as a distinct field of study. With his paper, an engineer had a relatively clear summary of what a very few scientists had come to know about the relationship between electronics and mathematics when applied to the idea of a thinking machine that could go beyond the simplistic functions of a slow tabulating device. The majority of his ideas sprang from work done in the United States during the period 1942–45, whereas the paper itself had a useful effect in the ten-year period after World War II.[34]

During the 1920s and 1930s others were also dealing with the increasingly obvious need to merge mathematics and electronics in practical applications. In France, for instance, Louis Couffignal published a series of papers in the 1930s in which he argued the case for presenting numbers in a binary form for computational machines to act upon. He devoted considerable attention to the description of how one might make a machine programmable, much along the same lines as had Shannon, Turing, and, later, Von Neumann.[35] Lesser-known scientists were arguing similarly at the same time.[36]

Thus, the science behind the computer is an example of information exchange across various disciplines that cumulatively led to the creation of sophisticated "high-tech" devices. The process began with developments in various scientific fields that were then blended at logical and attractive points and culminated in conceptualized and shared ideas that were discrete applications of science-based knowledge. Along the way, the efforts of scientists, mathematicians, and engineers intermingled, although early scientific research was the most crucial.

Advances in Technology

Developers of various lines of knowledge share their discoveries with colleagues by means of conferences, students trained, and papers and books published. As with the work of Turing and Shannon, published in journals that were available within the scientific community, advances in one field could influence events in others. During the 1920s and 1930s a number of refinements in various electronic components made possible some of the computational projects of the 1930s and early 1940s. Indeed, without a partial "off-the-shelf" approach, construction of ENIAC, Colossus, and other computers during World War II might not have been possible; certainly such tactics made that kind of construction easier in the immediate postwar period (1945–47) and, in both cases, quicker. At a minimum, it reduced the number of components that had to be invented for a particular system.

The need to calculate with greater quantities of numbers and data had stretched the limits of tabulating equipment during the interwar period. No community saw the limitations as clearly as the scientific world, which attacked the problem piecemeal with large calculating projects, advanced tabulating equipment,[37] and, in general, through experimentation with components that enhanced the capabilities of existing machinery. Work was done to improve, for example, the reliability of vacuum tubes throughout the 1920s and 1930s with impressive results.[38] These tubes, in time, would be components in the first memory devices for computers. Relays and switches became particular concerns, especially to researchers at Bell Labs during the 1920s and 1930s as they advanced the technical capabilities of telephone systems to handle long-distance phone calls in greater volume.[39] Network analyzers, used to determine the best way to move electricity through regions to customers, also required better wiring, switches, and components to monitor the flow of power and data with what were tantamount to analog computers.[40]

There was interest in the development of photoelectric devices that, in effect, could be employed in analog fashion. Truman S. Gray, at MIT, developed the photoelectric integraph, which was used to evaluate Fourier and superposition integrals.[41] Components were lashed together, for example, to create electrical counting systems faster than those available in tabulating or calculating equipment.[42] But work in the 1920s on components was hesitant when compared to that in the

1930s. In the thirties, major projects were under way at Bell Labs, MIT, various British and German universities, French institutes, and at large electrical and radio companies in the United States (e.g., General Electric and Radio Corporation of America, both of which had research laboratories). The products of these projects were very early protocomputational ancestors of the modern machine.

Indeed, during the 1930s a combination of electromechanical component developments and construction of devices were under way worldwide. Cathode ray tubes had been under development since the 1920s, for example, and substantially improved on both sides of the Atlantic during the 1930s to the point that immediately after World War II they could be used as memory devices.[43] Counters built for radios relying on vacuum tube technology improved upon earlier efforts from the 1920s as well.[44]

Most impressive was the number of machines actually built. It is traditional when writing the history of computers to describe the half-dozen or so major analog and, later, digital projects along with large calculating engines. A cursory survey of the literature from the period suggests, however, at least two dozen projects—many quite minor—in various stages of development in the late 1920s and early to mid-1930s. The lesser-known projects were evident both in the United States and in larger countries of Western Europe. All took advantage of a growing body of knowledge about electronics and electricity. In Great Britain, for instance, C. A. Beevers designed a special-purpose calculator that used sixteen electromechanical counters.[45] Clifford E. Berry, who was John Vincent Atanasoff's student while he was working on computational equipment, focused on advanced card-reading and -punching devices for computerlike applications at Iowa State College.[46] The British, as early as the mid-1920s, had already built a totalisator system that used electronic calculating devices to tally bets at races.[47] Leslie J. Comrie, the British mathematician, was also working on variations of accounting machines that could calculate.[48] At MIT a great deal of construction was going on that was better known. There, for example, Harold L. Hazen built a cinema integraph in the 1930s that evaluated integrals through analog means.[49] Throughout the 1920s and 1930s, however, his greatest attention had been focused on the design and construction of network analyzers for the electrical power industry.[50] A number of students of Bush and Hazen also worked on ancillary projects that exposed a generation of bright electrical engineers to the whole notion of using electronics for computing.[51]

Early projects using relays were evident outside the United States. No one yet knows what research and development programs were under way sponsored by European telephone companies, but limited evidence suggests that some individuals were active. For example, Bernard Weiner in Germany had pending a patent application in 1923 for an electronic computational device made out of relays with fixed built-in programs.[52] D. M. Myers designed a device in the late 1930s to calculate differential equations using an analog approach.[53] Others addressed the issue of doing differential calculations by using analog methods as well.[54] These projects were publicized only within the very small circle of interested scientists and engineers. But whether viewed from a European or American perspective, by the end of the 1920s efforts were being channeled toward development of relay, calculator, and analog machines. Especially during the 1930s, large calculating machines were built and, by the mid-1940s, so was the digital computer. Subsequent work on relay machines and analog computers was tangential to work on digital computing technology.

3

Analog, Electromechanical, and Digital Machines

During the interwar period, while advances were being made in the study and application of electricity, mathematics, physics, and engineering, results of such developments were being applied. More sophisticated calculators were built, a variety of analog devices were constructed, and by the end of World War II the first electronic digital computers were operating. These, in turn, were improved upon rapidly during the late 1940s and early 1950s and were commercially viable products by the mid-1950s. Historians have long noted the variety of projects under way, particularly during the late 1930s and throughout the 1940s. Perhaps most striking were the variety and quantity of activities that encouraged rapid developments, for example, in components and engineering, which, in turn, led to prototype machines. The central point made in chapter 2 and again through the case studies that follow is that a number of individuals and institutions moved from the theoretical to applied development of complex computational devices between the end of World War I and the early 1950s. They worked during a gestation period of some thirty-five years, but when finished, they had poised the technology so that engineers could take advantage of the new electronics that emerged from World War II. The ability of these engineers to develop practical machines rapidly between 1945 and 1955 at the start of a long period of economic prosperity once again facilitated the growth of organizations and fostered their need to handle ever-larger amounts of information. Prosperity made it possible for the U.S. government to fund the research infrastructures necessary to support projects not achievable by single individuals or too risky economically for private firms to assume alone.

I describe in this chapter the more focused projects that were recognized later as keys to the construction of commercial machines. These projects delineate a process of scientific and engineering interaction that led directly to application of such knowledge to specific problems. These projects are grouped along three lines of nearly simultaneous development: analog, electromechanical, and digital machines. More precisely, work on analog and electromechanical machines came before any significant activity with digital. The three sets of projects came so close together, often employing individuals comfortable in all three categories, that for my purpose here they can be considered simultaneous, almost integrated activities by a small community of individuals who were usually familiar with each other's work. The intimacy of concurrent activity was evident with many other technologies of the twentieth century as well, placing the pattern of behavior for computer inventors in the mainstream of technological advances.

Analog Developments

Important work was done in the United States in the 1920s and 1930s with analog devices. Yet analog equipment had been made in one form or another for more than two thousand years. Analog devices provide answers that are either approximations or ranges of data. For example, a slide rule gives an answer that is between two numbers, whereas a digital hand-held calculator gives the exact number answer. By the 1930s analog machines were considered useful for calculating differential equations, had already proven their worth in predicting ocean tides, had tracked movements of stars and planets between the two world wars, and were applied to management of power flows through network grids. Tide predictors had been the big success story with analogs; they had been in use since the late 1800s and were effective by the end of the first decade of the twentieth century.[1] Yet what was needed in the 1920s was an analog machine that could serve as a differential analyzer to solve, for instance, the problem of how to calculate the area under a specific curve.[2]

The earliest of the effective responses came from Vannevar Bush at MIT during the 1920s. He was trying to solve differential equations in connection with problems associated with a power network. Bush decided it would be more productive to develop a machine to do the mathematics involved than to attempt manual solutions through analytical methods. During the 1920s and 1930s he built machines that initially began with integrators, gears for constant multiplication, differential gears to perform addition and subtraction, and, finally, in the 1930s, gears operated by electricity. He used a combination of shafts and gears set for each problem. Although he constructed a number of machines, Bush built only two important generations of differential analyzers, copies of which were made for use both in Europe and in the United States during the late 1930s and early 1940s. They worked, and because these were publicized, his results were considered the most influential of the period. New uses were found for his machines, such as developing ballistics tables. Because he made his devices accessible to other scientists, engineers, and mathematicians for use in various projects, Bush indirectly encouraged interest in the possible use of computing machinery for solving scientific and engineering problems.[3]

Bush was not, therefore, the only individual interested in analog computing. Robert Dietzold[4] at Bell Laboratories, among others,[5] developed a machine to do algebraic calculations. Dietzold's associates at Bell Labs also had their own projects, the most notable of which was the isograph, an analog machine to do algebra.[6] Progress also came from John B. Wilbur of MIT, who illustrated how analog machines could be employed to solve simultaneous linear equations.[7]

In Europe similar work was under way to facilitate complex mathematics with analog devices. Most of the concern focused on development of machines that could perform algebraic calculations. Research was performed in Germany, France, Norway, and Great Britain, with important efforts centered at British universities.[8] Thus, as with other information-handling equipment, development continued as an international process, not an exclusive U.S. exercise.

By the time World War II began, analog machines were in use at various universities and laboratories in Europe and the United States although the majority of the estimated dozen or so devices were in the United States.[9] The Bush analyzer (as it came to be known) was the most widely used in the United States and certainly was the best known in the world. The Moore School of Electrical Engineering had one, for example, which its staff used to calculate ballistics tables for the U.S. Army.[10] Yet MIT remained the primary center of research and development for analog computers well into the 1940s.[11]

Perhaps even more important than how many analog devices existed and who used them was the effect such experiences had on future developments. Simply put, engineers who worked on Bush's analyzers or saw them gained knowledge about computing that encouraged or gave confidence to some who later developed digital machines at MIT, at the Moore School, and at other locations both in the United States and in Europe. The most obvious example of linkage between what was learned from Bush and what happened later was the analyzer that went to the Moore School. There it allowed some "hands-on" learning for engineers, a few of whom had elsewhere already developed an interest in mechanizing and electrifying complex computations. In addition to these individuals, many others (possibly as many as several hundred) either studied under Bush or visited his laboratory at MIT.[12] Bush did not hesitate to publicize his equipment through scholarly articles in the 1930s[13] and later exposed the trade press to his work as well. He even encouraged use of analog approaches over digital ones during World War II to the irritation of young engineers who thought they had a better way than analog.[14] Science had its politics too.

Mechanical/Electronic Calculators and Computers

Another line of development on the way to the modern digital computer (the type of computer most widely used after 1945) was a series of projects dating back to the 1920s and 1930s that relied on mechanical and electromechanical components and, to a large extent, owed their heritage more to calculators, tabulators, and telephone-switching equipment than to the advanced precepts posed by analog builders. But because the "mechanical monsters," as one historian called these very large devices,[15] were often underwritten by corporations and government agencies, they served as important learning exercises, perhaps in hindsight far more than did analog experiences. Immediately after these projects came the early attempts to build electronic digital machines. For that reason the history of large calculators and early digital devices is far more significant for the study of the American world of information processing than work done with analog machines.

Historians commonly think of several lines of development: Konrad Zuse's project in Germany in the 1930s, the work done at Bell Telephone Laboratories, the machines at Harvard, and a raft of projects at IBM—all before the advent of the digital computer. Although Zuse has received considerable attention from historians,[16] the fact remains that he did not influence any developments within either the U.S. office appliance industry or at any of the laboratories investigating computing within the United States in the 1930s or early 1940s. His work was not even known to either British or American engineers until at least the latter stages of World War II. By then the Allies already had major computer projects under way. Therefore, although Zuse's work was important within the context of post–World War II German computer history (because he formed a company to sell such devices, which became central to Germany's computer industry), his work was less consequential to the early history of computers in the United States.

The technology of the Bell Labs relay computer evolved very differently. First, like the various projects at MIT of the 1920s and 1930s, this was an R&D effort involving multiple teams of people sponsored by an institution. In contrast, Zuse built machines in his parents' living room with no institutional support and with the assistance only of a friend. Second, work on relay computers at Bell Labs was in response to specific needs, in this case to better the means to calculate when designing equipment to transmit telephone calls over long distances in greater volumes more reliably and less expensively. For those reasons, Bell Labs did both basic and, in the case of relays, applied research. It used scientific knowledge and an appreciation of existing technologies and parts to improve upon existing research and develop specific tools with which to operate the telephone system. Third, institutional support made possible complex projects beyond the realistic capabilities of one or two individuals, as was also true then with analog projects and in the 1940s and 1950s with digital systems.

By the 1930s the volume of telephone transmissions had become very large and sophisticated, requiring calculation of many and complex numbers when designing new switching systems. The work could not be done conveniently or quickly enough with just desktop calculators, hence the search for faster means. Without some assistance new telephone-switching equipment could not be developed quickly, and all the while dependence of the American nation on the telephone kept growing.[17]

At Bell Labs, George Stibitz (1914–), experimented in 1937 with relays, building a circuit that could add two single-bit binary numbers and generate results. The promise of being able to calculate complex numbers with such a gadget prompted Stibitz's manager, Dr. Thornton C. Fry, to allocate time and resources to the study of relays configured to calculate complex numbers. In typical corporate laboratory fashion, a project leader was appointed in 1938 (Samuel B. Williams), and engineers were added to the project over time because Stibitz was a mathematician not an electrical engineer. During the first quarter of 1939, Bell Labs arrived at a design for a machine. Williams and Stibitz began to build the calculator in April 1939, and by Christmas they were running trials on it. They declared the machine fully operational on January 8, 1940; the labs continued to use it until 1949. It should be noted that Stibitz rejected the electronic digital ideas of John Presper Eckert (1919–) and John W. Mauchly (1907–80) of the Moore School for his subsequent machines of the 1940s, preferring to build on the heritage of thought and experience in the Bell Labs community.

His first machine, the Complex Number Calculator, was the first built out of telephone relays and available parts. It could perform the four basic mathematical functions with complex numbers.[18] It also had three terminals attached to it. The machine proved useful as it exposed a number of Bell employees to electromechanical computing. Because a corporation managed the project and its officials worried about expenses, it was probably no surprise that executives at the labs balked at the final cost of $20,000 to make the device. Believing this price too steep, they elected not to construct any more copies.[19]

Observations about how the project was treated reflect patterns in computing history and offer insight into the evolution of industry-generated technology in the twentieth century. No doubt was ever expressed about the ability of the engineers to put together such a device. Indeed, one man had shown how simple the concept was. The experience of taking the machine from design to operation in such a short period suggests how simple it was once the concepts had been worked out. Given what was known about relay technology and computing at the time, the results were predictable, as evidenced by how the project was launched. Development was not an altruistic effort either. When officials saw that their expenses exceeded benefit, they did not hesitate to walk away from further development. That choice suggests that technological innovation at Bell was not always inevitable but came only when productive. When circumstances dictated otherwise (e.g., a project was paid for by the U.S. government), actions proceeded accordingly. That approach to technological innovation had occurred in the office appliance industry, too, and would be repeated many times in the computer industry after 1950.

Circumstances changed with the arrival of World War II. That conflict caused managers at Bell Laboratories to rethink the role that such types of machines could play in accomplishing a growing agenda of complex projects funded by the military community. Military advisors also encouraged the use of machines at Bell Labs and other locations. Bell employees became involved in government-sponsored projects, which made funding of calculation research easier to justify. Stibitz, for example, participated in the construction of an automatic aiming device for antiaircraft guns, which was sponsored by the National Defense Research Committee (NDRC). The design of that machine required large volumes of calculations to simulate its functions. For that purpose Stibitz chose to build an improved model of his earlier machine. Later called the Model II Relay Calculator, it was designed to perform linear interpolations and smoothing operations on data read into the system on paper tape. It became operational in September 1943 and had many of the primitive features seen later in digital computer systems: input/output devices, registers to store information, and the ability to execute up to thirty-one different instructions. The machine worked and was used by others as well. After World War II, Bell Labs turned Stibitz's machine over to the U.S. Naval Research Laboratory, where it continued to function until 1961.[20]

Stibitz and Bell Labs were involved in the development of other machines in the 1940s that were also based on relay technology. Models III and IV were constructed under similar circumstances: teamwork, formal support from Bell, the U.S. military for specific projects, and application to military and civilian problems. In each case there were no major breakthroughs in technology, simply more effective use of existing components made possible by the experiences gained on earlier projects or through slight improvements in existing parts, particularly those generated by the telephonic community of engineers. More capacity was added as well. Thus, for example, the Ballistic Computer (Model III), had twice the data storage capability of the Model II. The Model III was operational in June 1944 and in 1948 was moved to the Army Field Forces Board, where it functioned until 1958. The Model IV was completed in March 1945 for the navy and was used productively until 1961. The Model V and Model VI machines were also built during the 1940s.[21]

In each case (with the exception of the first machine), funding for construction of these engines came from military agencies with specific problems to solve. Engineers understood the required applications and appreciated how these would require more sophisticated calculating equipment. Bell Labs also recognized what it would take to make such devices and, therefore, sought funding assistance from outside its own budget. The knowledge gained by its engineering staff was then applied to the solution of Bell's own problems. The strategy of private industry supporting basic and applied research through government contracts became widely used during World War II and characterized almost every major technical development by industry in the computing field at least through the 1960s. Before work both at Bell Labs and at MIT, research relationships between government and laboratories working on computer-related projects had been limited. Cryptoanalytical work involving IBM tabulating equipment represented an important exception in the 1920s. By the end of the 1930s a relationship between government officials and researchers was forming; during World War II joint efforts became a major trend.[22] As a consequence, engineers increasingly depended on government funding, which, in turn, made possible more complex, expensive projects. The results increased the base of technical knowledge necessary for the creation of the computer.

A slightly different model of how research was handled in the 1930s and early 1940s involved the Harvard Mark I. Howard H. Aiken (1900–1973), a graduate student at Harvard in the late 1930s and later a professor there, wanted to combine registers and control devices to perform a long sequence of operations. To do the work required financial and engineering support. After the Monroe Calculating Machine Company rejected Aiken's proposal, colleagues at Harvard led him to IBM. A deal was struck whereby IBM would provide engineering and financial support (helped by the U.S. government) and build the machine of his design at its plant at Endicott, New York, in exchange for retaining patent rights. Aiken wanted to construct a machine, and IBM was interested in the prospect of an advanced calculator for its product line. The machine ran its first problem properly in January 1943, was moved to Harvard in February 1944, and was formally named the IBM Automatic Sequence Controlled Calculator (ASCC); Aiken called it the Mark I.[23]

The machine received considerable publicity, thanks largely to

Aiken's efforts. He also used it to train more than a dozen future computer scientists who worked either on this or subsequent models.[24] Although Aiken and IBM's Thomas J. Watson disagreed over who should receive credit for developing the original machine, its influence on IBM's engineers was more important.[25] Although technologically not as advanced as the ENIAC or, for a while, the Bell machines, it exposed IBM engineers to advanced computing methodologies and concepts. It encouraged IBM engineers to step beyond the ASCC to more advanced systems. During World War II vacuum tubes had become more reliable, and they wanted to apply such technology to an even faster calculator. The result was the IBM 603 Electronic Multiplier, which was first demonstrated to the public at the National Business Show in New York in September 1946.[26] It also influenced the Harvard staff and students, who later played key roles at Sperry, Raytheon, General Electric, Burroughs, and Honeywell in the 1950s and 1960s.

A variation in approach that delineates how U.S. military and government projects helped disseminate computer technology to office equipment manufacturers was the work of Ralph Palmer. He is remembered best for his deep involvement in the military's electronic computer projects during World War II and for introducing electronics and computer technology to IBM. Palmer worked for IBM at the start of World War II, joined the navy after the start of hostilities, and then spent most of the war working on computing projects, such as those under way at National Cash Register (NCR) in Dayton, Ohio, for the navy. While there, he learned a great deal about state-of-the-art electronics, which he wanted to apply to IBM's products after the war when he returned to the company. He linked up with others in the company interested in the new electronics, formed a group in Poughkeepsie, New York, to exploit this technology, and began experimenting with new methods of wiring, switching, counting, and so forth. The first product to incorporate the results of his naval experience was the IBM 604 Electronic Calculating Punch, first shipped in the fall of 1948. It could execute a minimum of twenty, and eventually up to sixty, plugboard-controlled steps, more than any other machine on the market. It had more horsepower than any other device. To produce it the company had to resolve a number of manufacturing issues; the experience served IBM well with other products that were significantly based in the new electronics. Historians of the digital computer consider the 604 pluggable circuit unit "a fundamental contribution to the art of digital electronic equipment design" for a variety of reasons. But the important point is the clear example of government research transferred through engineers back into private industry and then applied in ways that made sense commercially.[27]

The IBM 604 was bought in sufficient quantities to encourage IBM to pursue further the use of electronics, leading executives to support construction of faster calculators. In the late 1940s IBM began hiring a new generation of electrical engineers who were not burdened with the electromechanical/tabulating heritage of older IBM engineers. They constructed a series of new devices in the late 1940s that calculated at the speed of electronics, used components that came out of World War II, and were later enhanced at IBM, at other commercial laboratories, and at universities in the United States and Great Britain.[28] The most important of these new machines was the IBM Selective Sequence Electronic Calculator (SSEC), dedicated on January 27, 1948. It was the first device from IBM to combine the concept of the stored program with electronic computation and to operate on its own instructions as data. The engineers who worked on this project subsequently built the IBM 650, the most widely used computer of the 1950s (more than eighteen hundred were built). That kind of success kept IBM on the path to the modern computer that would become the basis for its business volumes.[29]

The third model of research and development in the United States and how it contributed to the commercial acceptance of computers concerned the overall interest of IBM in computing in general. As the largest office machine supplier by the end of World War II, it was obvious that whatever products IBM introduced would affect the industry at large. IBM as a company had learned over several decades that its most successful products met specific needs as perceived by customers and improved upon previous technologies to enhance efficiency, cost performance, and reliability. Furthermore, each product had to be profitable on its own merits. During the 1930s tabulating technology had increasingly been refined to handle more volume by supplying additional functions with decreasing human intervention and employing more and better electronic components. The whole process was successful for vendors and customers alike. During World War II normal evolution of product development slowed, but design work and growth in knowledge of new technologies sped up, especially as the result of rapid injection of appreciation of electronics into the firm (the work of Ralph Palmer). That, in turn, allowed IBM to move effectively into a series of products in the late 1940s that did more than simply manage data or tabulate. In short, IBM inched into the world of the computer in a cautious, evolutionary manner.

The emergence of the ASCC, then the SSEC, and, finally, the IBM 650 suggests the process. No wide-eyed technological radicalism was at work here, not even the boldness of an Eckert and Mauchly team striking out toward a new world of digital computers. Although the UNIVAC received enormous publicity in the early 1950s and its installation at the U.S. Bureau of the Census worried IBM executives long accustomed to thinking of that agency as a solid tabulator customer, the number sold would have registered the machine as a failure at IBM. Only when market demand was sufficient to beat the volumes of a UNIVAC did IBM effectively use its internal knowledge of computers to vie for the lead position in the new industry and not simply to block the UNIVAC from taking over the business of its key customers. IBM no longer relied solely on military contracts for economic incentives.[30]

Thus, the conservative quality of evolutionary product development is one worth examining further. At IBM, the early base for achievements with the SSEC and the IBM 650, for instance, grew out of work done on calculators and punched card systems developed at the Endicott Laboratory and in conjunction with research at the Watson Laboratory directed by Professor Wallace J. Eckert (1902–71) at Columbia University. The first complex machine that encouraged IBM to move into advanced computing was the IBM 601 Multiplying Punch, introduced in 1935. It was a relay-based device that could multiply two numbers in roughly one second. It proved so reliable that it became the standard machine of the late 1930s and early 1940s for both scientific and commercial calculations. By the time the product was retired, IBM had installed some fifteen hundred copies, a huge success by the standards of the day. A series of subsequent multiplying punches enhanced IBM's internal knowledge of computing while leading customers to depend on them more and, hence, to ask for enhancements. These machines included the IBM 602, 602A, 603, 604, and 605. The IBM 604 (introduced in 1948) was built using vacuum tubes, reflecting IBM's final departure from the less-reliable relay technology of the mid-1940s and showing that IBM was trying to market this computer as the evolutionary replacement of some multiplying machines that were numbered in the same way.[31]

The IBM case delineates in another way how information about technology flowed into a firm that ultimately would be a major supplier of computers. The example of IBM employee Ralph Palmer reflects again the interrelationship already pointed out that existed between business and government.

The question of what came first, demand or technological innovation, is one of real interest to historians of technology.[32] In IBM, demand more often than not drove technological innovation (at least in the precomputer era). The IBM 604 was a case in point. The need for increased reliability and cost-effectiveness led IBM engineers to shift to vacuum tubes once it had become obvious that this was a more reliable technology. That confidence came in large part from the experience of radio manufacturers and those involved in early computing projects (Palmer's group), all of which were publicized within the small circle of engineers and scientists working in the field.[33]

Customers came back for improvements. For example, Northrop Aviation requested that IBM lash the IBM 604 to an IBM 407 tabulating machine to generate printed results of scientific calculations rather than the traditional punched-card output. The IBM 407 printed results on standard accounting machine paper. IBM combined the two machines, added registers to hold additional data, and operated the configuration under command of a sequence of instructions from punched cards. Then IBM announced this new configuration as a product, the IBM Card Programmed Calculator (CPC). Although only two hundred were installed—it was very advanced for its day and, hence, useful enough to justify its price only to a limited market—it was as close to a computer as one could get in IBM's product line of older technologies and tabulating architectures.[34] The strategy was to lash together existing technologies, add some improvements, and approach data handling and calculations as a system (see Fig. 3.1). But the underlying assumption was, once again, that yet a little more function should be squeezed out of existing technology. The follow-on machine, the IBM 626, continued that strategy by offering more function and capacity but relying on the previously available architecture.

IBM, like MIT and Bell Labs, increasingly depended on government contracts to pay the cost of advanced research and development. IBM funded its own R&D for tabulating technologies because cus-

Figure 3.1. **IBM Card Programmed Calculator (CPC), 1948**

tomer demand was there to support it; commercial results confirmed the investment. Other projects, more tentative and therefore riskier, had to be funded from other sources. Increasingly, these other sources were government agencies. Reliance on government agencies to use the equipment was also obvious. The Harvard project was supported through a contract with the U.S. Navy, which agreed to finance its operation. The company made two IBM Pluggable Sequence Relay Calculators during 1944–45 for the U.S. Army to calculate ballistics tables at the Aberdeen Proving Ground. Others were subsequently built for the U.S. Navy. These machines used relay technology and IBM's normal plugboard organization technologies. This approach was incorporated in all of IBM's advanced tabulating products used to supply instructions to these machines in the mid-1940s. Relays connected or disconnected plugboards of programs. These devices calculated nearly ten times as fast as a normal IBM 602 Multiplying Punch.[35]

Experiences with these machines made it possible for engineers to develop the SSEC. The SSEC ultimately was a very important machine for IBM because its use was marketed successfully to commercial customers. In turn that experience justified for IBM executives the need to continue their investment (overwhelmingly funded through U.S. government contracts) in developing electronics-based products in the late 1940s. That kind of focus ultimately led to the IBM 701, introduced in 1951; it was the company's first electronic stored program computer.[36]

The pattern of evolution that had emerged by the end of World War II continued to govern many R&D decisions in the late 1940s. One line of development included technical advances in components and in one-of-a-kind devices at university laboratories, exemplified by the work done at MIT in the 1920s and 1930s and at the Moore School in the 1940s. A second line of concurrent evolution included construction of devices to solve specific research or customer requirements, as reflected in the work at Bell Laboratories and IBM. A third trend was extraction of technology from laboratories of the 1930s into government-sponsored projects, which resulted in technology disseminated into military and, later, commercial organizations during the 1940s and early 1950s. These projects were carried out by increasing numbers of people, who spread their knowledge throughout the American electronics and office equipment industries after World War II.

In the early to mid-1940s, for example, the staff at the Moore School grew as it built the ENIAC and, later, the EDVAC for the U.S. Army. After World War II, more than a half-dozen key engineers from the ENIAC project left to work on other computer endeavors around the United States.[37] Engineers at MIT first worked on projects concerning radar and training simulators, and later, hundreds were employed on the Whirlwind computer. Breaking codes in Great Britain with the Colossus helped to expand experience and diffuse skills into universities and companies at large.[38] In each case mathematicians, engineers, and physicists worked together during World War II. Alan Turing worked with engineers; John Von Neumann, the mathematician, served as consultant to engineers at the Moore School. Scientists advising the U.S. government directed research funds toward specific projects. Thus, Vannevar Bush, as an advisor to the U.S. government, and Herman H. Goldstine, as an army officer, forged links between computer builders and the government. Howard Aiken and Ralph Palmer served in the U.S. Navy during the war and, thus, built ties to that agency as well. Von Neumann was a consultant to both army and navy ordnance during and after the war, and, hence, had established such ties also.[39]

Development of Digital Computers, 1940s–1950s

Mainstream technological developments, in which the application of

newfound knowledge about computing and use of increasingly effective electronic components was most successful, came with the development of digital computers. This class of machines, first built in the
1940s, provided the necessary examples and technical experiences required to create devices (and soon after, software) that users could
reasonably rely upon to support commercial and scientific applications.
When these developments were coupled with economic incentives,
that is, both technical and price performance advantages of the new
equipment over tabulating and accounting machines, the economic
basis existed for the shift to new technologies. That came by the early
1950s, within just one decade from the beginning of serious and effective work on digital technology. Because digital equipment was so well
received, it became the technological bedrock of the data-processing
industry.

The "Golden Age" of computer science, the period in which many
of the basic concepts operative today came into existence, was the
eighteen years from about 1942 to 1960. In these years engineers and
scientists built and used the first digital computers and took enormous
strides in improving their reliability. All the while they fostered increases in both computation speed and the volume of data computers
could store in memory. This was also the era in which they originated
software to manage computer systems (made up of processors and
various input/output equipment) and to perform specific tasks (applications), such as generate payroll checks, control and track inventory, or
scan the skies for enemy aircraft.[40] Progress was sufficient to cause
executives in the office appliance industry to take notice, if at first
slowly, and to embrace the technology.

In 1945 and 1946 a number of projects were under way in the United
States to build computers, many sponsored by the federal government.
The same was true in Great Britain. During the late 1940s, additional
projects were started; some tentative work was done by commercial
enterprises. The hunt was on to improve technology and, in turn, all
devices associated with computing.[41] The story of the digital computer's
creation has frequently been told as a successful search for new technologies in the period 1945–55 and of its growing reliability and capacity.
It was also a period when scientists and engineers shared their discoveries openly. The resulting advances were unobstructed by patent considerations to the degree seen earlier in the office appliance industry with
tabulators and accounting machines, or later in the computer industry.[42]

The importance of the digital computer over older technologies can be highlighted by looking at speed and function. Scientists and engineers were already concluding by 1940 that calculations performed electronically could be done up to one thousand times faster than with more conventional electromechanical means, old desktop calculators and tabulating equipment of the 1920s and 1930s. By 1945 one could perform a multiplication on the Harvard Mark I calculator in about 6 seconds. This machine, not even a computer, was far more efficient than its electromechanical ancestors but slow when compared to its near contemporary, the ENIAC, which could do the job in 2.8 milliseconds in 1946. The ENIAC's drop of nearly two-thousandfold in processing time, although dramatic, was followed by another one-thousandfold decline in processing speed by 1960. Both the Harvard Mark I and the ENIAC cost essentially the same to construct, which suggested that greater efficiencies were attainable just by focusing on the nature of the technology used.[43]

During the 1950s increases in performance were achieved essentially by incremental improvements. Engineers tinkered with different components in various combinations within a computer system. This approach resulted in increases in the speed at which arithmetic operations could be performed first by one magnitude by the early 1950s and by yet another by the end of the decade. Important computers of the period and their speeds of operation listed in Table 3.1 suggest the improvements. The increase in processing speed was important because only with dramatic improvements was it possible either to displace tabulating and accounting machines of the past or to think of more complex uses for these computers, applications calling for calculations of much larger quantities of data.[44]

But in addition to processing speed, which could have been increased on analog devices as well, functional characteristics of digital computers were attractive. Since digital machines provided specific (numeric) answers, rather than analogous estimates (as did analog computers), they could be used for the kinds of commercial applications to which tabulators had been applied for nearly a half-century. Punched-card users needed a machine that could process more data faster in a manner similar to tabulators.

The digital computer had the potential to do that; in fact, that is exactly what happened. With additional speed and capacity, and, they hoped, lower costs later, one could perform analytical applications not

Table 3.1

Processing Speeds of Early American Computers, 1946–54 (seconds)

Machine	Year	Access Time	Addition Time
ENIAC	1946	0.001	0.0002
IBM SSEC	1948	0.001	0.0002
UNIVAC I	1951	0.0003	0.0005
IBM 701	1953	0.00003	0.00006
UNIVAC 1103	1953	0.00001	0.00003
IBM 704	1954	0.00001	0.000024
CAB 2000	1954	0.00001	0.00046

practical on punched-card equipment. These applications included "what if" analyses, operations research, advanced cryptoanalysis, creation of ballistics tables, and calculation of complex mathematical problems associated with meteorology and the development of the atomic bomb all requiring quantum increases in computing power over that of tabulators or calculators.

By 1944 or 1945, with the designs of the ENIAC and Colossus, engineers had some appreciation of what it would take to construct a digital computer. It then became increasingly a task of putting the pieces together, experimenting with various components. The critical technological problems, however, included how to build larger, more reliable memories and how to speed up processing in general. Memories, in particular, exemplify the problem of capacity. The ENIAC had a 20-word memory in 1946; the machine as a whole used 18,000 vacuum tubes. The Williams tube technology on the MADM computer at Manchester University (1948) took fast memory capacity up to 32 words. But that was not enough. The UNIVAC I (1951) had a capacity of 1,000 words; the IBM 701 (1953), 2,048 words; and the IBM 704 (1954), up to 8,192 words. Only with such increasing amounts of memory could one hope even to begin performing useful applications. The requirement for additional processor memory kept growing over the next several decades, encouraging developers to add more memory but scarcely keeping up with the demand.[45]

Engineers also had to worry about the speed of the components involved and focused on improving these at the same time as they expanded the size of memories. The types of technology used on major systems of the 1940s and 1950s and the strides made are shown in

Table 3.2. Again, as with other aspects of a computer's construction, the strategy employed was initially to build machines using components available during World War II and later use advances in parts. The first devices relied on vacuum tubes, then mercury delay line memories. Both had proven their worth in various electronic devices (such as radar and radio). Smaller vacuum tubes appeared by the end of the war but, like their predecessors, they were hot, unreliable, used too much electricity, and remained far too bulky. Engineers increasingly turned to mercury delay lines to provide faster and more reliable components. These converted electrical pulses to sound waves that traveled through tanks of mercury and then were reconverted into electrical pulses. Sound waves traveled slower than electrical pulses, and, thus, information could be stored in such tanks before being reconverted into electrical pulses. But these devices were too delicate and unreliable. An additional deficiency was the fact that they operated serially.[46] Another approach, developed largely by British workers, was the use of the cathode ray tube (CRT). The inside of a CRT was painted with an electrical charge, making it possible to warehouse information briefly in a manner that made access random rather than sequential. But it, too, was an unreliable approach because the coating of a tube's interior glass wall with phosphor was uneven. The CRTs had to be refreshed constantly with more electrical pulses. Furthermore, the tubes were very large and took up too much space, looking very much like the tube screens from either a very bad space movie of the 1950s or newsreel footage of an air traffic control room.[47]

Computer builders increasingly turned to magnetic storage mediums to solve the problems of capacity and reliability. Harking back to the recent experience of the 1930s and 1940s with magnetic recording tape, engineering groups applied the same principle in the postwar period to magnetic drums, which, although slow, appeared far more reliable than vacuum tubes, mercury delay lines, or CRTs. The initial slowness of such devices, coupled with still too-limited capacity, meant that computers were not yet functionally very useful. The final evolution in memories that made possible widespread computer use came in the early 1950s as part of the project to build Whirlwind for the military at MIT. Jay Forrester (1918–) at MIT, An Wang (1920–90) at Harvard (founder later of Wang Laboratories, working on memory systems), and Dudley Buch and Jan Rajchman (1911–) at RCA each developed, almost independently of the other, what came to be

Table 3.2

Technologies of British and American Computers, 1940s–1950s

Machine	Year	Technology
ENIAC	1946	Vacuum tubes
IBM SSEC	1948	Electromechanical and electronic components
EDSAC	1949	Mercury delay lines
UNIVAC I	1951	Mercury delay lines
EDVAC	1952	Mercury delay lines and drum
Whirlwind	1950s	Magnetic core
IAS Computer	1952	Flip-flops and CRTs
IBM 701	1953	Williams tubes
IBM 704	1954	Ferrite cores
IBM NORC	1955	Williams tubes

Note: Most machines of the very early 1950s were also bit serial design devices or of mixed serial/parallel design.

known as magnetic core, or ferrite, memories. Rings of ferromagnetic substances (which looked like doughnuts) with wires strung through them were used to establish the direction of magnetic flux. That magnetic flux represented a piece of data. Larger, more efficient core memories followed during the 1950s and 1960s in the United States, which made possible more reliable flow of data in memory at electronic speeds.[48]

As memories were being improved, logic circuits of greater reliability and speed were also essential. There were no useful answers until after development of the transistor. Since the last days of World War II, work had been under way at Bell Labs to find a substance that could transmit electronic pulses over long distances by amplifying their power from point to point. Engineers suspected that the use of semiconducting materials (such as germanium or silicon) might provide the answer. Then, in late 1947, they developed a crude device out of a nonconductive crystalline substance into which impurities had been introduced. Electricity flowed through the impurities along a particular path. In effect the substance could operate as a switch and an amplifier. Its advantages for computers were many. It was small, used little power, had no moving parts, and proved far more reliable and less expensive to build than earlier technologies. It took AT&T and Bell Labs to perfect the transistor to the point where it could be used in a computer.[49]

The U.S. National Bureau of Standards' Eastern Automatic Computer (SEAC) was the first machine to use germanium diodes (an early semiconductor) for its logic along with vacuum tubes. Built in the late 1940s and operational by the end of 1950, the SEAC proved the effectiveness of these new electronic components. During the 1950s, computer designers increasingly relied on transistors and diodes to enhance the power and speed of their devices.[50] The other important development was the shift from germanium to silicon diodes by the early 1960s. This change was initiated, at first, to increase speed, not to lower costs, because silicon components were more expensive than germanium-based transistors. But silicon proved more cost-effective.

Another advance needed in the 1940s was the development of larger magnetic storage for data over and above the memory actually housed in a computer. In Table 3.3 major milestones in this arena are cataloged. In lay terms, computer builders needed storage capability to warehouse increasing amounts of data, which could be accessed directly and quickly. The storage had to be auxiliary to the computer much like 80-column cards were to tabulating equipment. This would allow a user to store millions of pieces of information outside the computer to be used only when needed. Ideally they wanted the computer to find this information too. Main memory in computers could not do the job because it was so expensive in comparison to punched cards for tabulating gear. Although a number of new input/output devices were developed to move data in and out of computers (such as the use of tabulating cards and input/output peripheral machines made by various vendors and attached to computers), the need for magnetically stored and managed data that could be moved about reliably at high speeds was required to balance systems that were acquiring increasingly faster memories, storage, and logic circuits.

Initial work by Engineering Research Associates (ERA) on behalf of the U.S. government in the immediate postwar period led to creation of the first magnetic drums used in computers in the United States. Others began to work on this kind of technology. IBM acquired responsibility for further enhancing the drum under a series of U.S. government contracts during the early 1950s. By the mid-1950s it had developed the first commercially available magnetic disk drives for peripheral storage of data. That event, along with the increased use of magnetic tape, which had been available in various forms and at several speeds since the 1930s, began to address the needs for fast storage.

Table 3.3

Early Computer Memory Systems, 1941–59

Era*	Type	Sample of Computers Used On
1941–44	Relays	Harvard Mark series
1945–47	Thermal	Never implemented
1940–50	Mechanical	Zuse machines
1946–53	Delay line	EDSAC, EDVAC, UNIVAC I, LEO I, Pilot ACE, SEAC
	Electrostatic	Whirlwind, IBM 701, IAS
1947–50s	Rotating magnetic	ARC, IAS
1952–59	Static magnetic	Whirlwind, IBM 704, IBM 7090

*Dates are approximate and subject to debate because not all computers were converted to new technologies at the same time and different combinations were often used during their lives.

Tape drives were improved throughout the 1940s and 1950s, offering users sequential access to data directly attached to processors. With disk drives came direct access to specific pieces of information stored on collections of platters that looked much like stacks of phonograph records.[51] By being able to go directly to a piece of information rather than having to read an entire file preceding a desired record (as on tape), one could process information faster. The initial disk storage device was available in prototype from the National Bureau of Standards in 1951, but in 1956 IBM introduced the first computer system that actually relied on disk drives for auxiliary storage (IBM Type 350 magnetic disk system for use with the RAMAC 305 computer).[52] From the 1950s through the 1980s, faster, more reliable tape and disk drives were developed that could also handle greater volumes of data.[53]

All of these developments reflected applied research building on existing technical advances and experimentation with principles of electricity and materials and new configurations of devices. This research was done both at university laboratories (1940s and 1950s) and, increasingly, at corporations (by the late 1940s and early 1950s), usually funded by federal contracts and grants during the 1950s. By the 1960s the commercial viability of these technologies made it possible for corporations to assume an increasing portion of the R&D costs from the U.S. government to improve upon these machines while still seeking federal support for cutting-edge research, for example, time-sharing, networking, and advanced graphics.

Yet the final piece of the puzzle required from the technical and scientific community before the digital computer could become commercially viable involved development of software, programs that would make use of the computer possible. The late 1950s and early 1960s are frequently called the Golden Age of software because during that era many of today's high-level programming languages emerged along with some of the earliest major operating systems, in effect also unleashing market forces that influenced subsequent development efforts.[54]

One could, however, just as easily argue that developments in the 1940s and 1950s in software were at least as important. By World War II notions about information processing had evolved sufficiently to identify the need for and basic functions of instructions to a computer. Without the initial efforts in software, use of the computer would not have been possible, let alone practical. The list of things that had to be developed during the first generation of computers (1940s to 1950s) became the basis for much software in subsequent decades. For example, computer users needed instructions for applications, to move data in and out of computers, to command associated equipment, to execute instructions, and so on, all within a computer system. In the beginning a user had to describe these tasks in great detail. Engineers had to have profound knowledge of how such systems worked; programmers did too. The "programming" (also called "coding" from the earliest days) was in low-level language code in terms directly intelligible to the computer and usually was fed to machines in the form of punched tabulating cards. This low-level programming feature of computer use characterized the entire decade of the 1940s. As the 1950s dawned, however, computer scientists had already started to search for language-like tools that could be used to do the job, relying first on algebraic notation and then on alphanumeric symbols such as English words or combinations of letters, numbers, and symbols. Armed with a translator or compiler, one could, in theory, translate English-like commands into terms intelligible to the computer. The development of programming languages in the late 1950s was a successful attempt to accomplish part of that task. By the 1980s several hundred new languages were coming into and passing out of existence each year; about one thousand were in actual use around the world.[55]

In addition to programming languages to instruct computers, operating systems were required: bodies of programs that managed a computer system, thus freeing a programmer to write application software (e.g., payroll, accounts receivable, defense networks, airline reservations). Programmers wanted to stop having to instruct the computer how to go to disk files for data, for example, merely to note what data to get. Table 3.4 highlights some of the major events in the early history of software. The data in the table suggest that the first generation of software—as well as the first generation of hardware—gave direction to the next four decades of developmental activity.[56]

The bulk of the major "events" in the development of the digital computer occurred either in the United States or, to a lesser extent, in Great Britain. Important machines included the ENIAC (1946), followed by its successor at the Moore School, the EDVAC (1951), SEAC (1950), SWAC (1950), the Harvard Mark III (1949) and Mark IV (1952), the UNIVAC I (1951), which was the first of the widely publicized commercially available systems in the United States, the 1101 (1950), Whirlwind (1951), IAS (1952), and the IBM 701 (1952) and IBM 702 (1955). As a group, these machines represented the first wave of computers built in the United States in the period 1946–53 and, in effect, set the direction for research and development for years to come.[57] During the period from 1953 to 1959–60 the first major commercially attractive systems within the industry appeared, suggesting the effectiveness of R&D's incremental improvements over older systems. The most widely employed machines of the late 1950s included the all-American-made machines: IBM 650 (1954), the IBM 700 series (704, 705, 709), the UNIVAC II (1957), and entrants from Burroughs (205, 220), NCR (120, 200), Datamatic (1000), and RCA (BIZMAC).[58]

The ENIAC was built primarily as a result of the leadership of John W. Mauchly and John Presper Eckert. Their work led next to the EDVAC, then to the BINAC (1949), and, finally, to the UNIVAC series. These systems spawned a whole line of equipment. More forcefully than any other group of engineers, Mauchly and Eckert also made computers publicly acclaimed tools for business, science, and government.[59] Less dramatically, but in the long run more effectively, engineers at IBM evolved their company's product line from tabulating equipment to digital computers through dozens of product announcements, beginning in the mid-1940s. Their efforts—with much guidance

Table 3.4

Major Events in the History of Software, 1940s–1950s

Event	Year	Comments
Flowchart developed	1946/47	By Goldstine and Von Neumann
Plankalkul	1940s	Described by Zuse
General-purpose subroutines	1945/50	Machine-level instructions
Composition	1948	Code-generating algorithm
SHORT CODE	1950	First high-level programming language
Bohm's Compiler	1950/51	Early pseudocompiler
Publication Wilkes's *Preparation of Programs*	1951	For EDSAC
AUTOCODE	1952	One of first compilers
A-O	1952	One of first compilers
Operating systems	1950s	Developed by General Motors
SCP[a] IBM 701	1955	Considered one of first SCPs
SCP IBM 704	1956	An early SCP
Mark I DB[b] IBM 702	1956	An early DB manager
MATH-MATIC UNIVAC	1956	Widely used high-level language
FORTRAN developed	1956	By Backus
FLOW-MATIC UNIVAC	1958	Widely used high-level language
9 PAC DB IBM 709	1959	Early DB manager
SCP IBM AN/FSQ7	1959	Major advance in SCP design

[a]SCP = system control program (operating system)
[b]DB = database manager to manage large machine-readable files

from marketing—unintentionally encouraged a process that culminated in the retirement of tabulating products by the dawn of the third generation of computers (mid-1960s).[60]

In Great Britain government projects influenced British computing on a more limited basis but in much the same way ENIAC did in the United States by spreading knowledge of such devices to various universities and government agencies in the immediate postwar period.[61] Maurice V. Wilkes, relying on his wartime experiences with radar and radio, represented another tradition in British computing. He built the EDSAC (1949) at Cambridge University.[62] Other computer projects were under way in the late 1940s at the National Physical Laboratory (NPL), Cambridge University, and at Manchester University.[63]

These British projects paralleled similar ones at American universities in this postwar period. MIT's Whirlwind was one example; another was Von Neumann's project at the Institute for Advanced Study (IAS) near Princeton University, where in the late 1940s and early

1950s, he built one computer. At various state universities, computer-building projects also started in the late 1940s and early 1950s.[64]

If one steps back from the story of the digital computer's development, several patterns become evident. First, work relied heavily on use of previous knowledge and experience with other technologies and components. Second, institutional and funding support was crucial and came largely from universities and, especially, government agencies. Third, corporate activity followed an intimate link with universities and government agencies until sufficient customers were available to translate these various special projects into products. Most impressive for the development of technology is how the computer was so closely intertwined in the activities of organizations in both public and private life. Although the roles of individuals (e.g., Von Neumann and Mauchly) were still important, they, too, had to work in teams and within institutions. Therefore, understanding the research environment engineers worked in becomes a crucial element in appreciating how technology evolved in the twentieth century.

This assessment of how information flowed among developers of technology is also useful as a possible approach for understanding how it occurs in other areas of research. The fact remains that historians know too little about the research environment's effects on the process of technology transfer.

Research Environment

The argument that development of the modern computer was made possible by advances in science (e.g., knowledge of electricity) and then through effective use of increasingly more reliable and efficient components (e.g., vacuum tubes, transistors, and so forth), supported mostly by government funding, by itself does not reflect the complete reality of what happened in the United States or even in Great Britain. Historians just do not know enough to extend the observation as confidently to events in France,[65] Germany, Italy, Japan, or the Soviet Union. Clearly, another facet of the period included generous sharing of information among early pioneers concerning their projects in a positive and willing manner that they felt benefited their own work.[66] That exchange of information, in particular during the 1940s, sped up development work. This was a process not yet encumbered by, for instance, concern over patent rights to the extent it would be beginning in the 1950s, when companies increasingly sought patent protection over R&D. The only exceptions, and they were merely momentary, were during World War II when war-related projects at, for example, MIT and the Moore School in the United States were kept quiet. But with the war's end, as with Aiken's work at Harvard, these kinds of projects in America began to receive considerable attention from the general press. Within the scientific community a similar process was under way that as much reflected a new subject enthusiastically approached as it did a topic that did not yet have the support of societies, organized committees, or a cadre of recognized "leading" experts influencing events and agendas. To some extent, however, the emerging new group did share some influential people—Stibitz and Von Neumann, for example—but they were very few and far between on both sides of the Atlantic. During the 1930s Shannon and Turing studied or described computational problems while others readily publicized their devices and projects. Bush published in the scientific press and entertained many visitors to his laboratory in an open fashion.

In December 1940, John W. Mauchly met John Vincent Atanasoff at the annual meeting of the American Association for the Advancement of Science where they shared their mutual interest in designing analog and digital computers. Mauchly subsequently visited Atanasoff in June 1941 where he saw what progress had been made on construction of a device called ABC. In 1946 a patent controversy developed over who invented the digital computer, Atanasoff or Mauchly, with the former arguing that the latter copied his ideas in constructing the ENIAC. The argument also engaged many historians in subsequent years. The controversy, however, is not important to the history of computers because the ENIAC was built and used; the ABC was not. What was very natural in 1941, however, was for two men interested in computing to share their thoughts openly with each other.[67]

A review of the literature published during World War II suggests that a slow-down in public knowledge of computing occurred but not a shutdown of all information among government-supported engineers during the war.[68] The U.S. Army's Ballistics Research Laboratory (BRL) and the Moore School shared information as the ENIAC was being built from 1944 on.[69] Von Neumann kept in touch with American engineers working on various computing projects as well.[70] Immediately after the war ended, information sharing spread quickly; in fact, in his memoir/history of computing, Goldstine devoted a whole chapter to the phenomenon, entitled "The Spread of Ideas."[71]

The Moore School, which in 1946 was on the verge of making ENIAC fully operational and already designing EDVAC, hosted a series of lectures and tours to which engineers came from the Institute for Advanced Study, the NDRC's Applied Mathematics Panel, and MIT's Servomechanism Laboratory to visit. RCA had its research laboratory at Princeton, New Jersey, not far from Philadelphia, and so shuttled back and forth, sharing some of its fundamental technology while the Moore School also entertained visitors from the Theoretical Physics Division of the Los Alamos National Laboratory.[72] Forrester came from MIT and later went on to build the Whirlwind. Von Neumann, of course, had been a frequent visitor and later constructed a machine at IAS.

The British also came to the Moore School but, in addition, toured other locations that had computer projects. Goldstine specifically attributes the direct development of computers in Britain to these visits to the Moore School, however.[73] What he may not have fully appreciated at the time that he wrote his book (published in 1972) was how far the British had already gone toward developing computational devices as a result of wartime code-breaking activities, war projects that were still shrouded in secrecy by law. Maurice V. Wilkes, father of the EDSAC at Cambridge University, came to the Moore School and acknowledged its influence on him as well.[74] British visitors also came from the National Physical Laboratory (NPL), which later built ACE, and from Manchester University, later home of the Manchester Mark I. Douglas R. Hartree and Leslie J. Comrie, two well-known experts on mechanical aids to computing, also viewed the ENIAC.[75]

Besides these visits in 1945–47, the Committee on Mathematical Tables and Other Aids to Computation of the National Research Council sponsored a conference on computing equipment on October 29–31, 1945, at MIT. Some of the organizers included Comrie, Aiken, and Stibitz, with others representing the University of Liverpool and the Moore School, thus assembling the first international conference on the subject. Attenders included John Grist Brainerd, Eckert, and Mauchly, all from the Moore School, and Von Neumann and Goldstine on behalf of the U.S. military ordnance community.[76] Another major event to grow out of ENIAC was a class run by the Moore School in the summer of 1946 called the "Theory and Techniques for Design of Electronic Computers," funded by the army's ordnance department and the Office of Naval Research. It surveyed the then-current knowledge about computing in the United States. Wilkes attended the class and prized its contribution to his own work on the EDSAC back in Great Britain.[77]

Additional information was exchanged at Harvard University. Professor Aiken had established a laboratory to study computation. In 1946 his staff at the laboratory published *A Manual of Operations for the Automatic Sequence Controlled Calculator*.[78] Those interested in computing studied this manual because it represented one of the first to describe in detail how to solve numeric problems using a computer/calculator-like machine; in effect it was the first programming manual. During the late 1940s Aiken hosted two conferences on the subject in which he brought together students, professors, engineers, scientists, government officials, and others from both sides of the Atlantic to discuss computing. He thereby influenced, in particular, European computer builders more than did Eckert and Mauchly at the Moore School before they left to form their own firm in the late 1940s. The symposium held at Harvard on January 7–10, 1947, reflected concerns of the period.

In that year perhaps a dozen or so major computer projects were under way, which involved fewer than one thousand people.[79] So it was still a small community of interested persons, operating mainly in universities and helped by government funding. With no structure yet to the new field of computing, engineers knew they were operating in near isolation and welcomed exchanges of information, one of the few options available when the usual support structures for a field (e.g., societies, specialized journals, formal annual conventions and conferences, etc.) did not exist. What little flowed into printed form appeared in fewer than fifty journals, most publishing on the subject only occasionally. Some of the established scientific societies paid little attention to the new field. For example, the Franklin Institute, long a bastion for the established scientists (including Bush and Hazen) did not publish on digital computers. Those that did included the Institute of Radio Engineers (IRE), the American Institute of Electrical Engineers (AIEE), and the Mathematical Tables and Other Aids to Computation (MTAC).[80] Regular computer conferences did not begin in any organized fashion until December 1947, eight years after extensive work had begun with digital computers and some twenty-five years after the beginning of modern analog computing. The Eastern and

Western Joint Computer Conference began in 1951 and the National Computer Conference in 1953. By the end of the 1950s organizations were also forming to help computer engineers and scientists.[81] Thus, the ad hoc sessions at Harvard were important. The 1947 conference held by Aiken was the third major event in the yet nascent world of American computers; the first two were MIT's conference in 1945 and the course at the Moore School in 1946.

The conference at Harvard included a tour of the laboratory to show off Aiken's machines and then several sessions of papers.[82] Forty people gave papers; they represented Harvard, MIT, the University of Pennsylvania, IAS, New York University, the National Bureau of Standards, the Naval Academy, Ballistics Research Laboratory, Bureau of Ordnance, Naval Ordnance Laboratory, Naval Proving Ground, Office of Naval Research, Eastman Kodak, Electronic Control Company, Brush Development Company, RCA, and the Centre National de la Recherce Scientifique of France. In the audience were 152 attendees from 86 colleges and universities, 90 from government agencies, and 75 from private companies. The total number of those attending represented perhaps one-third of all those active in the computer field in the United States. Some sessions surveyed existing calculating machinery, large-scale calculators, storage devices, numerical methods and problem solving on hardware, and programming; other sessions focused on input/output equipment, and discussions were held on various design problems.[83] Harvard sponsored another conference of almost equal importance in 1949; IBM had done the same the year before.[84] Cambridge University held its own in 1949,[85] and Manchester University followed in 1951,[86] the same year that a number of major publications appeared on computing.[87] Organized events later in the 1950s reflected a routine. A milestone in the United States was the formation of the Association for Computing Machinery (ACM) in 1947, which, during the 1950s, established a series of events and publications that supported the computing scientific community for decades. Its first major conference came in December 1947; publication of its official journal began in 1954. It has served as a major outlet for discussion of technical computing topics to the present.[88]

But what was it like for researchers working in the new field in the 1940s and 1950s? Conferences obviously were important stimulants because they allowed them to learn, exposed them to fresh thinking, and helped them establish personal contacts in a new field of science and engineering. Memoirs hint how these people felt. An Wang, who worked at the Harvard lab and later became an important developer of computer memory, noted, "Those of us working on computers in the late 1940s enjoyed the sense of purpose and the creativity of the times, but I suspect that most of us did not have a sense that we were making history."[89] He added, "I believe that the open relationships between the labs in the United States and Great Britain, and the absence of government secrecy, sped up the pace of discovery. Perhaps this is why the computer flourished here rather than in Soviet Russia."[90] Wang called the period of the late 1940s the most creative in the history of computer science, an era when "researchers speculated openly about what a computer should look like and what it should do."[91] In short, young developers appeared more enthralled with the technical thrill of success than by economic opportunity.

Maurice V. Wilkes also echoed Wang's thoughts, "We saw computers as coming to play a central role in both science and business."[92] He found the summer class at the Moore School especially useful because "the lectures amounted to a pretty comprehensive canvassing of the various ideas then current."[93] In fact, he recalled returning to Great Britain "with my head full of thoughts for constructing a stored program computer."[94] As in the United States, visitors turned up at each of the computer projects. At Cambridge University, Wilkes was to note later, they "had plenty of visitors to the Laboratory who wished to find out what this new subject of computers was all about, but there were very few people who were already sufficiently informed for it to be possible to discuss technical issues with them on equal terms."[95]

Of course, actual research and construction were not easy. "There was much spade work to be done in order to turn a raw computer into a useful tool," commented Wilkes.[96] Attendees at the Harvard lectures made the same point.[97] The Moore School's summer course was significant precisely because it dealt with that issue.[98] An attendee at the Harvard conference noted that because he and so many others learned how to improve their R&D activities, the session "became the springboard for subsequent computer conferences."[99] The excitement of change and discovery was in the air. Herman Lukoff, who worked on developing what became the UNIVAC, recalled that "we knew we were doing things that had never been done before,"[100] and with very long hours "without the slightest thought about overtime pay, which the company couldn't afford anyway."[101]

Similar enthusiasm and frustrations applied to programming. John Backus, the father of FORTRAN, the most widely used scientific programming language for nearly four decades, recalled life in the early 1950s:

> Programming in the America of the 1950s had a vital frontier enthusiasm virtually untainted by either the scholarship or stuffiness of academia. The programmer-inventors of the early 1950s were too impatient to hoard an idea until it could be fully developed and a paper written. They wanted to convince others. Action, progress, and outdoing one's rivals were more important than mere authorship of a paper. Recognition in the small programming fraternity was more likely to be accorded for a colorful personality, an extraordinary feat of coding, or the ability to hold a lot of liquor well than it was for an intellectual insight.[102] An idea was the property of anyone who could use it. . . . As in any frontier group, the programming community had its purveyors of snake oil. . . . The success of some programming systems depended on the number of machines they would run on.[103]

The strategy of the period remained for all engineers in hardware and programming, as it had in the 1930s, to construct systems using enhancements to existing ideas and components with perhaps a dash of new thought. Julian Bigelow, who worked on the IAS computer with Von Neumann, recalled that in 1946 and 1947, as the team was beginning to form at IAS, management laid down a strategy for development: "We decided to use standard available parts as best we could or find out why we could not." That approach sped up production.[104] Engineers specialized on test equipment, recording media, or circuit elements.[105] Even with a sophisticated, nearly well-staffed project such as Whirlwind, invention on the fly was still required. One participant in the project remembered that there was "no technical infrastructure . . . as we know it today. There were few instruments. We had to go ahead and do almost everything for the first time and when I say we I mean not only the Digital Computer Laboratory but everybody in the computer business." He cited the problem that "tube life characteristics were unknown," yet the practical reality governing their lives was "the double thrust for speed and reliability in a real-time machine."[106] Thus was the computer revolution brought about.

Conclusions

If one were to look for deep and profound insights into the evolution of technology by examining what happened in the initial stages in the development of the computer, disappointment might follow a search for dramatic breakthroughs or quantum leaps forward. This form of technology developed as had so many other "high-tech" strands, through a slow process of unassociated scientific discoveries accumulating over time followed by individuals versed in aspects of science applying the principles they understood in some practical manner. Their initial efforts were, then, "optimized" to enhance existing technologies, either their components or the thinking that produced them, before being forced by new circumstances to rethink, reconfigure, and rebuild new devices for new uses. To a large extent that pattern dictated the flow of events in the creation of the modern computer. In fact, even the term *invention* is inappropriate because the ultimate machine was a product of many avenues of work and changed as time passed. For example, the configuration of the Whirlwind or of the earlier ENIAC evolved as new memory types were added or subtracted, and as new combinations of software and input/output equipment were tried over the years.[107] Even today that process continues; it is witnessed each time a vendor's field engineer comes into a data center with engineering changes to install—either in the form of new components routinely attached, or as microcode to make a system even more efficient, or to correct problems already identified. The point is that the configuration of a computer system never remained static in the 1940s, 1950s, or later; it was always in flux.

It is very obvious that patterns of behavior in the precomputer era influenced the epoch following 1955. As scientific knowledge grew, individuals seized it in an attempt to solve practical problems. So many ideas and fields of knowledge had to come together to make the computer possible that, with a vision of what ultimately had to be built as the incentive, R&D projects became more than single-person activities. Projects were adopted by ever-growing staffs at laboratories such as those of MIT, the Moore School of Engineering, IBM, AT&T, GE, RCA, IAS, and elsewhere. The process became so complex that the U.S. government had to farm out the work to already established laboratories and to finance almost all of it. The U.S. Navy turned to Aiken and his crew at Harvard and to others at NCR, and the U.S. Army to the engineers at the Moore School. Every military organization underwrote projects at MIT and even after the war supported such organizations as the National Bureau of Standards[108] and ERA to do the work.[109] Unlike in the 1960s and 1970s, when significant and substantial R&D had shifted to commercial laboratories, during the 1930s to 1950s the main stages for development were universities, closely linked to government agencies. Office and electronics vendors merely played support roles.

Another feature of computer R&D was speed of development. Although scientists took centuries to acquire sufficient knowledge to make the computer a reality, they moved with alacrity in the late nineteenth and early twentieth centuries. This process of accumulated momentum included improvements in the understanding of electronics, machining and packaging, information science, and physics. Thus, in the early decades of the twentieth century a more focused mission emerged, namely, to find mechanical and electronic means to calculate and manage data in large volumes. What comes through clearly is the speed of development: independent, almost eccentric activities in the nineteenth century; analog projects with results in the twenty-year period between World Wars I and II; and creation of the first of several digital computers in less than five years in laboratories. These events were followed by other projects requiring less than one decade to complete. They focused on enhancing and making more efficient and cost-effective (thus commercially viable) a new generation of machines. By about 1955 that process had progressed sufficiently for new agendas to be set that would influence both engineers and vendors for the next three decades, among these agendas were development of higher-level programming languages, operating systems, integrated circuits, disk drives, and telecommunications.

The process was not simple to execute when it came down to individual projects, as early computer builders commented. These people hoped, cooperated, were interested, and always felt that opportunity lay around the corner. The enthusiasm that Lukoff said made it acceptable to work long hours, skip meals, and deal with components that did not always work well characterized how progress was made. If that mind set contributes to the general understanding of how technology evolves in general, so be it, because similar patterns were evident later when, for example, minicomputers were built by small teams or microcomputers were developed in dormitory rooms at Harvard University and garages in California.[110] Software remained an art form at least to the 1960s,[111] to the great consternation of hardware veterans who thought they had figured out how to invent or improve upon older machine-based technologies.

When examining what happened to the data-processing industry as it evolved during the 1940s and 1950s, one is hard pressed to avoid the conclusion that the kind of basic functional innovations that emerged were prerequisites to any commercial opportunities to sell computers. The market issues of what to sell and to buy had to begin with a product, one that could be sold and acquired for advantageous economic reasons in the middle decades of the twentieth century. Scientists and engineers had to lead the way, which they did. Their initial efforts go far in explaining why funding for such work had to come for individuals like Aiken, who worked with IBM's engineers to build new machines. Another exemplar was Goldstine, who convinced the U.S. Army to fund complex projects for Mauchly and Eckert. Faith in the work of young engineers was very clearly part of the story. Defense contracts supported Eckert and Mauchly on the BINAC, the U.S. Navy encouraged creation of ERA, MIT remained tied to government agencies for funding (as with Whirlwind, the most expensive computer project of its day).

As discussed in chapter 4, business executives were doubtful at first about the new technology when it meant risking the fortunes and fates of their firms. They were, however, willing to explore the possibilities of a new faith. Although initially skeptical, once converted, they proved most effective in spreading the new gospel.

1. IBM plant, Poughkeepsie, New York (1948), home of early computer R&D at IBM (IBM Archives).

2. IBM 650 (1953), the most widely used commercial computer of the 1950s (IBM Archives).

3. UNIVAC I system (1954), the most widely known commercial computer of the 1950s (Charles Babbage Institute).

4. John von Neumann and the ENIAC (1946) (IBM Archives).

5. Thomas J. Watson, Jr. (1955), president of IBM in the 1950s when the company began selling computers (IBM Archives).

6. J. Presper Eckert (ca. 1950s), codeveloper of the ENIAC and UNIVAC (National Museum of American History).

7. John Mauchly (ca. 1950s), codeveloper of the ENIAC and UNIVAC (National Museum of American History).

8. IBM 650 being assembled at the Poughkeepsie plant (1953) (IBM Archives).

9. An early example of vacuum tube technology applied to an IBM calculator (1946) (IBM Archives).

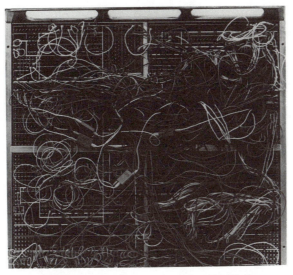

10. The control panel of an IBM 407 accounting machine (1949), "programmed" by wiring various parts together as were other machines of the late-1940s and early-1950s (IBM Archives).

11. An early example of a military-sponsored computational device, the Harvard Mark I (also known as the IBM Automatic Sequence Controller Calculator [ASCC] in 1944 (IBM Archives).

12. A military inspired computer, the IBM 701 (1952) (IBM Archives).

13. The SAGE system (1956) (IBM Archives).

14. The IBM 705, which grew out of military computing support (1954) (IBM Archives).

15. The RAMAC 305 (1956), the first commercially available system with direct access storage files (IBM Archives).

16. The Control Data 1604 (1959) with Seymour Cray (famed super computing architect) at the console (Charles Babbage Institute).

17. The IBM 701 (1952). Computers were "packaged" early-on as attractive systems. (IBM Archives).

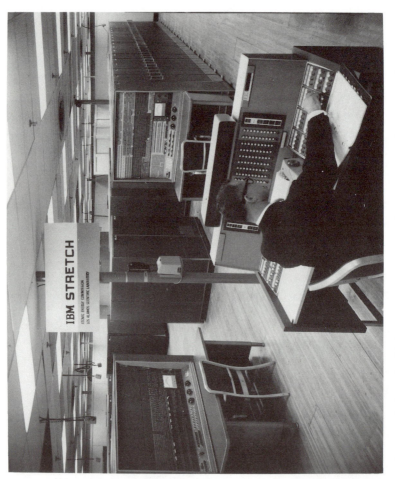

18. The IBM 7030 (STRETCH) system (1960). By 1960, "packaging" had style (IBM Archives).

19. IBM 705 tape drives (1954). Tape storage was an important early part of all computer systems (IBM Archives).

20. A computer center in the late 1950s (IBM Archives).

21. An IBM 26 (1949). The most widely used data entry devices for tabulating and later computer equipment from the 1930s through the 1960s were key card punch machines to "punch" data onto computer cards (IBM Archives).

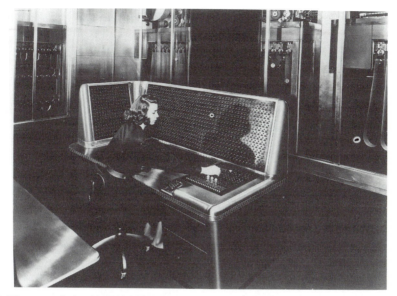

22. The console for the IBM SSEC (1948). This is what a computer looked like to Americans in the 1940s through the 1960s (IBM Archives).

23. An IBM 608 in 1955. A computing device using transistors (IBM Archives).

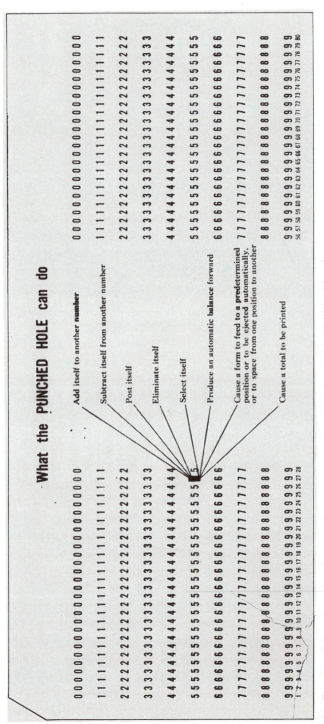

24. The 80-column "computer" card that was developed by IBM in the 1920s (IBM Archives).

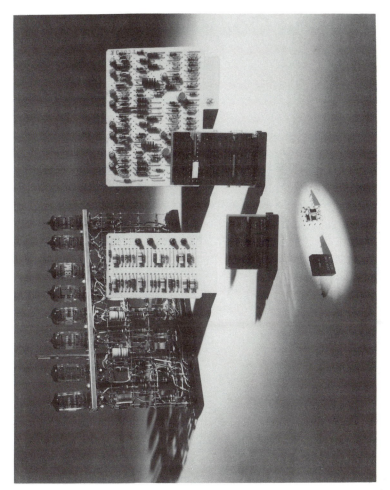

25. Three generations of computer technology—vacuum tubes (1940s), transistors (1950s), and silicon-based "chips" (1960s)—all packaged as they would appear inside computers (IBM Archives).

4

Vendors' Initial Responses to the Computer

Expanding the bounds of scientific knowledge and technologies is one thing, but seeing them adopted as commercially viable products is quite another. Since the late 1860s, office equipment technologies have been embraced first by vendors to sell and then by customers to buy, but only when both parties had confidence in the usefulness and reliability of these machines and after they proved more cost-effective than existing technologies. So it was again during the early days of the computer. The history of the computer's adoption by customers was not marked initially by wild enthusiasm, although interest was always considerable. Developers faced many serious stumbling blocks, including customers who had little notion of how or why to use such machines, and the enormous cost, size, and complexity of computers.

Students of the data-processing industry have struggled with a confused picture as well. It is very common, for example, to read histories of the computer that focus on characteristics of early machines and how they were built, yet give little attention to how many users there were or, in some instances, in which applications they were employed. Technical histories also deal with how computers became involved in computing by stressing how far back in time corporate interest existed in computer products.[1] But one should not confuse interest in electronics with the actual shift to computer-based products; these were two distinct events. The first involved normal evolution of interest in newer technologies as a way to enhance existing product lines (as at IBM), providing an incentive to change some existing products. There was interest in adding a potential new line of offerings to an existing product set without necessarily displacing the old (as at Remington Rand). Some firms were attracted to computers when a newly formed company offered the new technology in what essentially was a niche market in the late 1940s and early 1950s (ERA, e.g., or the Eckert and Mauchly enterprise).[2] Many of the small specialized firms were eventually acquired by more established ones; a number of well-known electronics companies (GE and RCA, for instance) studied computer technology and added such products to their lines. The giants of the office appliance industry did the same when it became obvious to their executives that these were the waves of the future that would wipe out their existing products. They were all, however, always cautious and tried not to damage their current revenue streams from older technologies (e.g., IBM, Remington Rand, NCR, and Burroughs), and they were not always successful.

Therefore, to put the early history of the computer's acceptance into better balance, one must sufficiently distinguish technological developments from customer or vendor acceptance to observe that the story is far more complicated than has been portrayed. It involved interplay of evolving scientific interest with some cautious product introductions that yielded both marketing and engineering lessons. It is also a story of business finally reaching a set of customers who, nervously at first and more confidently later, migrated to the new devices. One must differentiate the published hype about the benefits of computers from actual practice. For example, it was very common in the late 1940s and early 1950s to see articles in popular magazines and revered business journals in which the benefits of computers were discussed. But at the same time more than 90 percent of IBM's revenues, for instance, came from tabulating equipment, not from the new electronics.

The traditional view of the industry's adoption of the computer is a simplistic tale of two major vendors, IBM and Remington Rand, emerging quickly out of the initial flurry of computer-related efforts of the late 1940s to compete for a new market. IBM and Remington Rand are pictured as the two office equipment colossi fighting in the early 1950s. Remington Rand was favored initially, but IBM ultimately won the contest for market share by the mid-1950s. Indeed, both became major suppliers of computers by the late 1950s, participating to a large extent in the few computer sales made at that time.[3] But that view, reminiscent of two American cowboys shooting it out on a dusty main street at high noon, misleads because many companies in the office appliance industry and, generally, in the field of electronics, struggled with whether or not to enter the fray with their own computer products. Many represented potentially serious rivals to IBM and Remington Rand. These included AT&T, GE, and RCA. A small cluster of new computer companies focused their sales toward scientific and engineering communities not regularly serviced by traditional office appliance vendors or electronics manufacturers.

Market receptivity was always a major concern and cost-effectiveness of products an issue. Any one of these "other" firms might have become the computer industry if they had been more serious rivals of IBM and Remington Rand, if they had invested in these technologies, and if their pricing had been aggressively attractive. But those issues belong to the post office appliance era and to the history of the data-processing industry proper. The point is that initial receptivity for computers by both vendors and customers was simply not clear-cut. Furthermore, rivalry between IBM and Remington Rand was not necessarily obvious when it came to computers until the UNIVAC appeared in the early 1950s. At that point the two-decades-old competition between the two firms heated up once again.[4] To complicate matters further, companies such as RCA and GE already had computing products as impressive as those at either IBM or Remington Rand. Thus, the response to the arrival of the computer was varied, often hesitant, and never very clear before the mid-1950s. For firms in the electronics field it was a new world. For the office appliance industry it became a new chapter in a market's history, one already more than sixty years old.

The only detailed corporate responses reviewed in this book are those of IBM and Remington Rand, and those of several smaller, new computer manufacturers. IBM and Remington Rand, between them, manufactured more computers than all other suppliers in the early 1950s and clearly came to dominate computer sales by the end of the decade. Thus, their successes exemplify the process of a high-technology product going from laboratory to market and not just two vendors shooting it out on the main street of a new market. I recognize that this "office equipo–centrism" runs the risk of biasing the view of the early industry; my intent, however, is less to present a full history of the industry than to describe how technology generally moved from laboratory to market. In the end the old office equipment vendors still came to own the lion's share of the new computer business.

Table 4.1

Sample of Major Computer Technologies Supported by the U.S. Government, 1946–61

Event	Year	Remarks
Stored program concept	1946	EDVAC
Plastic magnetic tape	1950	BINAC
Error-correcting code	1950	Bell Labs
Microprogramming	1951	Whirlwind and M. Wilkes
Magnetic tape drive	1951	Remington Rand
Interrupt mechanism	1953	ERA
Graphics display	1953	Whirlwind
Core memory	1953	Whirlwind
Rotating magnetic memory and storage	1950s	ERA
Hydrodynamic air bearing	1956	RECOMP and SAGE
Redundancy	1957	SAGE
Transistor components	1950s	TX-O, 7090
Instruction pipeline	1961	Stretch
Multiple arithmetic units	1961	Stretch

Source: Data drawn from Kenneth Flamm, *Creating the Computer: Government, Industry, and High Technology* (Washington, D.C.: Brookings Institution, 1988), Table A-1, 260–61, Table A-2, 262.

Note: Some major exceptions to government funding included floating point at IBM (1955), and input/output processors (data channel) at IBM (1958).

The Role of Government and R&D Support

In a carefully prepared study of the data-processing industry's relations with the U.S. government, Kenneth Flamm of the Brookings Institution showed that nearly every major technological development before the 1960s was either funded by the U.S. or British governments.[5] Furthermore, many computers before the late 1950s were financed initially by the government and then sold to government agencies. The role of government support was overwhelming, and that of commercial customers nearly nonexistent (see Tables 4.1, 4.2). As late as 1959, one U.S. government study suggested that 85 percent of research and development in electronics conducted in the United States was being paid for by various government agencies.[6] Many important electronics and office appliance firms in the United States participated in the computer game under contract to the U.S. government in the postwar period. Leading funding agencies included all the military services (particularly ONR), the National Bureau of Standards (NBS), many

Table 4.2

Sample of Major Computer Projects Supported by the U.S. Government, 1945–61

Project	Year	Remarks
ENIAC	1944/46	U.S. Army
SSEC	1948	Military
SWAC	1949	NBS, construction began
BINAC	1949	Military
Whirlwind	1950	Military, partially operational
UNIVAC I	1951	U.S. Bureau of the Census
MANIAC	1952	Los Alamos Lab
IAS	1952	IAS Project
IBM 701	1953	Los Alamos Lab
DYSEAC	1954	U.S. Army
IBM 650	1957	Military support
IBM 7090	1958	Military support (partial)
ERA 1101	1959	U.S. Bureau of the Census
LARC	1960	Lawrence Radiation Lab
STRETCH	1961	Los Alamos Lab

Note: Many other computers existed, such as the ILLIAC, ORDVAC, and NORC.

cabinet-level departments, and the Atomic Energy Commission. In fact, many initial technologies, in particular, and various computer introductions continued to be funded in one fashion or another by the U.S. government into the early 1970s. This approach remained despite the enormous growth in commercial computing in the 1960s that provided significant justification for computer vendors to fund their own research with nongovernment dollars (e.g., IBM S/360 and S/370 computer families).[7]

The government supported research on software (e.g., for SAGE, LISP, and ALGOL, RAND and SDC on JOVIAL). Initial operating systems required more connection to government support because they were necessary to make computers actually work. Many advances in software during the 1950s, however, made computers easier to use by commercial customers. Of the thirteen most important early programming languages (as defined by a panel of computer scientists in the 1970s) only four depended on federal funding.[8] Flamm's research, however, suggested that overall the U.S. government played an important role before the 1960s (see Tables 4.3, 4.4).

Flamm argued that "it was no accident that the military services largely financed the postwar development of the computer in the

Table 4.3

Software Receiving U.S. Government Support, 1946–63

Development	Year
Flow charting at IAS	1946
Whirlwind operating system	1954
SAGE time-sharing system	1957
First use of virtual memory	1961
MIT CTSS system	1962
SDC Q-32 time-sharing system	1963
Carnegie RJE system	1963
JOSS	1963

Source: Adapted from material in Kenneth Flamm, *Creating the Computer: Government, Industry, and High Technology* (Washington, D.C.: Brookings Institution, 1988), Table A-4, 266–67.

Table 4.4

Major Programming Languages Receiving U.S. Government Support, 1950s–1965

Government-supported	Year	Remarks
Languages		
APT	1956	MIT Whirlwind
COBOL	1959	Department of Defense support
JOVIAL	1959	Department of Defense
Basic	1965	NSF support involved
Assemblers, Loaders, Compilers*		
First compiler	1952	For weapons research
First algebraic language	1953	Whirlwind
First assembler	1956	SHARE assembly program

Source: Kenneth Flamm, *Creating the Computer: Government, Industry, and High Technology* (Washington, D.C.: Brookings Institution, 1988), adapted from material in Table A-4, 268–69.
*Elements often associated with languages.

1950s, for computing technology had played a pivotal role in the Allied war effort."[9] Initial commercial machines were adaptations of devices built first for the military. Some of the more obvious examples of this pattern at work are listed in Table 4.5. For reasons of national security the government had to continue supporting research because electronics firms proved reluctant to make large financial commitments to new technologies: some firms were very small, and some

Table 4.5

Commercial Computers Derived from U.S. Government-sponsored Research, 1950s

Machine	Year Shipped	Remarks
ERA 1101	1950	U.S. Bureau of the Census
UNIVAC I	1951	U.S. Bureau of the Census
ERA	1953	Evolved from 1101
IBM 701	1953	Defense calculated
DATATRON	1954	Electrodata-Burroughs
IBM 702	1955	Grew out of IBM 701
IBM 704	1955	Used SAGE technology
BIZMAC	1956	RCA/U.S. Army project
IBM 705	1956	Used SAGE technology
D-1000	1957	Raytheon military project
UNIVAC	1958	Grew out of UNIVAC I
IBM 709	1958	Grew out of IBM 704
IBM 7070/7090	1959	U.S. Air Force project

lacked confidence that the return on their investments would be profitable. In fact, the government's investment was significant, as high as 85 percent of all R&D funding for EDP at the time.[10] Given the size of the expense for R&D in electronics already by the 1940s and 1950s, many electronics/office firms were reluctant to assume such financial burdens.

Thus, the pattern that emerged was one of government agencies commissioning commercial organizations to research components and, then, to construct equipment. Commercial enterprises agreed to cooperate because government projects were profitable and allowed them to acquire expertise in what many perceived to be the wave of the future at little or no expense to themselves. After a particular R&D effort had been completed, and, for example, a computer had been delivered and installed at a government location, these firms sometimes attempted to develop commercial versions. For instance, the IBM 701 and 702 and Remington's UNIVAC I came from military heritages.[11] Basic research remained with universities, applied research with commercial organizations. Worldwide, the U.S. military dominated funding of computer research.[12] Flamm estimated that by 1950 the U.S. government alone was spending between $15 million and $20 million each year on computer-related R&D.[13]

One of the by-products of this funding was the creation of start-up firms during the early to mid-1950s to chase military dollars. For all eighty U.S. suppliers of computers in the 1950s, the U.S. military was their single largest customer, followed by defense contractors.[14]

Through the 1940s and 1950s a small group of computer companies supplied government agencies and scientific users. In this early period they were very important because the firms that later would come to dominate computer suppliers were barely interested, still committed to the sale of more traditional product lines. Start-up computer firms thus loomed large on the computer scene up to the mid-1950s, primarily supplying the military and noncommercial users. The existence of these vendors first made possible the early packaging of computer technology into devices, and second, nurtured applied computer science. In time, some of these firms would be absorbed by other companies interested in acquiring computer knowledge quickly. The early computer companies were receptive to such acquisitions because they usually were starved for the capital needed to bring to market computers still under development.

A quick example of an early start-up was Engineering Research Associates (ERA). Supported by the promise of U.S. Navy contracts, a team of naval personnel who had worked on cryptography during World War II formed the company. Its two earliest founders, Harold Engstrom and William Norris, set up shop in St. Paul, Minnesota. They built machines for cryptological purposes in the late 1940s, developing along the way substantial expertise in magnetic drum memories, a technology that eventually appeared in many general purpose computers in the 1950s. In 1947 ERA began to build its first digital computer. Called the Atlas, ERA delivered it to the U.S. Navy in 1950. ERA tapped R&D under way at MIT and at various government agencies to speed the development of this machine. After the SEAC, theirs was the second electronic stored-program computer in operation in the United States. The ERA 1101—the firm's first commercial product—was a variation of the Atlas. Flamm has estimated that ERA built "80 percent of the dollar value of computers sold in the United States through 1952," making it the largest computer vendor of its day.[15] In 1953 ERA shipped its first ERA 1103. By then Remington Rand had acquired the firm. The experience of Eckert and Mauchly (builders of the UNIVAC) paralleled the story of ERA.

Thus, in that early period between 1945 and, roughly, 1953, several sources of computer development existed in the United States: government agencies, such as the National Bureau of Standards (NBS) and the U.S. Navy, with various projects; a raft of universities, such as MIT, Harvard, Stanford, and the University of Pennsylvania, under contract to the U.S. government to do R&D; and variety of start-up firms such as ERA. All had connections to each other; none operated in isolation.

One other pocket of activity, in historical hindsight, looms in importance as a transporter of computer technology from laboratory to market. Located on the West Coast of the United States and tied closely to the aerospace industry in Southern California, which, in turn, was very dependent on government contracts, this activity focused on scientific and engineering computing.[16] The design of aircraft inherently required extensive mathematical calculations, as did applications such as missile guidance. Early efforts (late 1940s) were primarily housed at Northrop Aircraft and to a lesser extent at Raytheon. Both had projects funded by the U.S. government: Northrop for its Snark missile and Raytheon for a naval control processor, for example. Northrop worked with an instrument supplier (Hewlett-Packard) on early digital projects. Then, in 1950, a group of Northrop engineers formed their own computer company called Computer Research Corporation (CRC). Like ERA, it had a military sponsor the U.S. Air Force for which it built various computers in the first half of the 1950s.

In 1953 NCR bought CRC. Both at Northrop and at CRC engineers knowledgeable about computer technology began to migrate to other firms: Bendix, Logistics Research Corporation, Packard-Bell, and Scientific Data Systems, among others. Caltech engineers familiar with computers also dispersed to other firms—such as Consolidated Electrodynamics Corporation (CEC)—in the early 1950s, thus disseminating knowledge of computers.[17] On the West Coast, Hughes Aircraft, North American Aviation, TRW, and the Rand Corporation all worked on military and scientific/engineering projects through the late 1940s and early 1950s. Flamm clearly identified the pattern of information diffusion: The key element in these efforts was the fluid movement of talented engineers from one aerospace patron to another and into start-ups that often survived only long enough to be acquired by a larger firm. In the long run the activities of these aerospace-based firms led to the development of the minicomputer.[18]

The consequences for the future were substantial. This heritage of scientific/engineering computer development spawned a large number of firms in the 1960s and beyond while it fortified the computer skills of many existing companies. Coming out of this sector, and not from the office appliance world, were such companies as Digital Equipment (1957), Control Data (1957), Cray (founded in 1973 by former CDC employee Seymour Cray), Data General (1968), Datapoint (1968), and Prime (1975), to mention just a few. The nonoffice appliance heritage has continued. For example, all of Japan's indigenous computer suppliers (not including IBM Japan) grew from vendors of communications and industrial equipment, beginning in the 1950s.[19] Thus, the temptation to think that only IBM and Remington Rand spawned an industry bankrolled by the U.S. military community would be a gross display of office equipo-centrism even though IBM, for example, came to dominate the large mainframe business by the early 1960s. This dominance was challenged effectively by the 1980s by vendors of mini- and microcomputers who had different heritages.

Central to all vendors, however, was the role of the U.S. government. In fact, the overall importance of the U.S. government's role in these early years would be difficult to overstate. In the years after World War II a debate continued within the government on its role in industrial development.[20] But when one examines specific computer projects, one sees less economic theory at work and more pragmatic approaches to problem solving. The various military agencies appear to be almost independently seeking alliances with start-up firms to continue meeting their needs, while continuing links to established corporations. The NBS came closest to comprehensive computer R&D support; their approach most closely reflected the Japanese model of subsequent years. The Japanese invested significant amounts of public funds in their computer industry in the 1960s and 1970s in proportions similar to funding in the United States by the late 1950s and early 1960s.[21]

American projects were always highly focused. Marie Anchordoguy, in her excellent study of the Japanese computer industry, concluded that the Japanese experience, on occasion, exemplified "the limitations of industrial policies when they target vague goals in areas where few have any expertise and when they are not structured in ways that require firms to become more competitive over time."[22] Yet, as in the U.S. case, the Japanese government was willing to absorb the early costs and risks of R&D to launch a new industry. In both instances the process worked. One major difference, however, was that the Japanese government sought next to limit "the number of players in each market segment to promote economies of scale in R&D and production,"[23] whereas the U.S. government encouraged many vendors and a spirit of competition.

Reaction of Vendors to Early Computer Research and Development

Companies that had an interest in computers uniformly followed a strategy of continuing support primarily for their traditional lines of business in the 1940s and into the 1950s. Larger firms paid some attention to electronics in general in the belief that such technology could ultimately be applied to traditional product sets. The thought that such research would eventually lead to development of commercial computers did not gain any significant support until the early 1950s, and even then required a number of years before being realized effectively through introduction of commercially viable products.[24] In short, traditional office and electronics firms did not wildly embrace the new machines; they simply paid attention to the new technology.

At Burroughs Corporation, for example, as late as November 1951, executives believed that the study of advanced electronics, although important, would continue to influence current lines of products for a "period of 10 to 15 years."[25] There was no wide swing to computers in 1951 at Burroughs. In fact, executives there believed that "mechanical accounting machines along 'traditional' lines are likely to be the largest single factor in the business machine field as far as it is feasible to look ahead."[26] The problem for Burroughs, as for other firms, was that despite progress, "neither the size [n]or cost aspect have as yet been resolved at all satisfactorily."[27] Yet at the time Burroughs was spending about 25 percent of its research dollars on basic research (not all on electronics) and the rest on applied work in improving its product lines. The other reason for looking at Burroughs was its broad product line, which ranged from desktop adding machines to complex accounting machines. Pressure to fund development and marketing of these products was probably no less intense than, say, at RCA, with communications, radio, home appliances (e.g., television), and later, computers. A similar wide spectrum of products (e.g., jet engines and steam turbines) influenced events at GE and, to a lesser extent, Philco.

Thus, Burroughs is instructive. Most research there involved development of advanced products, punched-card machines in particular, in hopes of challenging IBM's supremacy in that field. In fact, one employee of Burroughs recorded at the time that "one of the most promising new fields for Burroughs, and perhaps the most keenly guarded secret, is in the area of punch cards."[28] The company joined the British Tabulating Machine Company (at one time associated with IBM but not since the establishment of IBM World Trade in the late 1940s) in an attempt to develop faster, less-expensive products than those offered by IBM for the European market. Burroughs invested in a subsidiary called the Control Instrument Company in hopes of going after tabulating gear (not computers) in 1951. An analyst at the time noted: "Clearly at this stage it would be advisable to adopt a wait-and-see attitude to the chances of Burroughs in the punch card field. IBM now has 85% of the market and Remington Rand has perhaps 5%. However, if Burroughs succeeds in breaking into the punch card market it is perfectly conceivable that the Company might build up a $100,000,000 business in punch cards alone."[29]

Control Instrument Company's work in leading-edge technology was being done at the request of the U.S. Navy and the U.S. Air Force at the same time that it was asked to work on punched cards.[30] Thus, again, commercial applications of R&D were privately funded, whereas questionable, possibly risky (from a commercial perspective) leading-edge work received funding from the government or did not get done. The reason for Burroughs's strategy of paying for its own commercial research but not for computers was clearly the result of the belief "that perhaps 70% of all office machines made 5 to 10 years hence may include some electro-mechanical features, with an annual market of $750,000,000, 20% may be small mechanical models, and 10% of the large UNIVAC type."[31]

For nearly forty years many of Burroughs's attitudes and practices mimicked those of other office equipment vendors, and its reaction to the computer was no different from those of other major suppliers. Differences were more of degree and timing. Burroughs's story helps put that of IBM and Remington Rand into correct context within their own market. IBM, NCR, and Remington Rand were some of the major office equipment suppliers also active in advanced research in the late 1940s and early 1950s. The history of IBM's early computer technology suggests a growing commitment to advanced electronics at IBM (or, at least, at the Poughkeepsie, New York, laboratory and plant) in the late 1940s and early 1950s.[32]

Yet even at IBM, the jump to computers was slow. Traditional accounts of the company speak of Tom Watson, Jr., a pilot coming home from World War II enthralled with electronics, using his power to swing the company over to this field in the 1940s and, in the early 1950s, into the world of computers.[33] William W. Simmons, an IBM executive who was a sales manager in the late 1940s, recalled that the company sold advanced calculators, such as the CPC, successfully in the period but that everyone in the firm "continued to think of computers primarily as scientific and engineering machines for the government and defense contractors."[34] Simmons went on in the 1950s to plan future products at IBM and found that despite the success of the IBM 701 as a military project (to help in the Korean War) that machine "seemed to confirm that computers afforded limited opportunities and were a sideshow when compared to the punch card accounting machines the company was turning out by the thousands to meet the needs of what was clearly its mainstream customers: the ordinary businessman."[35] Even after the U.S. Bureau of the Census took delivery of a UNIVAC I (which caused consternation at IBM because the bureau had long been a solid IBM customer), Watson's response was "aimed at what IBM considered the primary markets" for computers: "scientific and military computation."[36] This was a good marketing decision, yet as the 1950s progressed, of course, IBM's commitment to computers increased to the point necessary to make it successful in the new field. Simmons's portrait of Watson's reaction to computers and to that of his company as a whole is more consistent with the firm's market-driven perspective, which had existed since its founding days and remained evident in the decades after the 1950s. Watson's view is also compatible with the kind of reactions seen in other firms at the time.

In the 1940s and early 1950s at Remington Rand, similar concern about the viability of the computer for commercial customers slowed R&D funding other than what could be acquired for development of machines at the Univac Division[37] and by ERA on behalf of the U.S. government.[38] ERA, for example, although it sold machines commercially, relied on government funding for its R&D. For that matter, funding for computer development in general at Remington Rand came from the government or was not done until the early 1950s. The UNIVAC series of machines, beginning with the predecessor BINAC and EDVAC, were government projects, whereas ERA's role was to continue feeding advanced electronics to the U.S. Navy.[39]

Bell Telephone Laboratories produced computers for the U.S. government in the late 1940s after having begun internal development in the late 1930s. All of Raytheon's expensive computer projects of the 1940s were funded by the U.S. government. Unlike ERA, Raytheon did not have excess dollars with which to pursue commercial versions of its machines. In 1955 it joined the Minneapolis-Honeywell Regulator Company (thereafter called Honeywell) to develop a commercial machine ten years after the end of World War II and several years after IBM and Remington Rand had already made products available. Although much has been written about the failure of many firms to invest in computers in the early 1950s because they failed to recognize the market (at least in the United States) whereas IBM did see it,[40] the fact remains, as in the case of Raytheon, that significant quantities of research funds to support necessary work were lacking. One runs the risk of overstating the role of IBM and Remington Rand in these early years (1945–53). In this period both firms were, like other companies, shipping machines to scientific and government clients. IBM's early computer business focused entirely on such customers and only later shifted to commercial clients, as did other vendors. In fact, although IBM and Remington Rand dominated the commercial market by 1955–57, government-focused manufacturers sent commercial computers to market first; ERA made commercial computers available in the early 1950s.

Similar tales could be told about the roles of RCA, General Electric, NCR, and Philco. These firms either perceived a small market or saw scientific and government customers. All of these firms and their customers were supported financially by the U.S. government. Thus, much of the research and development by these companies in the late 1940s and early to mid-1950s was a function of government spending. This explains to a large extent why many of these companies did not begin to introduce commercial versions of previously built government machines until the late 1950s. They spent the late 1940s and early 1950s inventing machines for the military and various agencies and did not deliver them until the 1950s, entertaining commercial projects only afterward. Government investment also accounts significantly for the more rapid and extensive computer development in the United States than anywhere else.

The Role of IBM

The role of IBM is important because by the end of the 1950s it had

become an important provider of computers to most markets worldwide and held the premier position within the commercial market for
decades. The company was, by the late 1940s, no longer a small firm
by U.S. standards. Sales in 1945 generated total revenues of $141.7
million; gross revenues reached $214.9 million in 1950 and $734.3
million in 1956. By then IBM had more than 2,300 development engineers and was experiencing enormous overall growth in employee
population. For example, between 1954 and 1956, employment rose
from 50,225 to 72,504 and kept growing throughout the rest of the
decade. IBM's employee population at the end of World War II had
been approximately 22,000.[41]

IBM's people were scattered across more than one hundred sales
offices (called "branch offices") in the United States, several regional
marketing headquarters and many more district offices, major laboratory and manufacturing facilities at Endicott and Poughkeepsie and
fledgling locations elsewhere, and at corporate headquarters in New
York. Outside the United States, IBM owned manufacturing facilities
in Europe and in Asia and was marketing equipment in nearly eighty
nations. Thus, in any year after World War II it would have been
unrealistic to think of IBM in monolithic terms, to generalize about the
company as if all members of the firm were acting in complete unison
even if in public the firm spoke as if it were one voice. Yet writers on
the company have generally found it convenient to think of IBM in
such a fashion.[42] By changing the monolithic perspective of IBM one
comes closer to understanding the various currents of opinions and
actions that existed not only within this company but across the industry at large.

Because of size alone, one could argue that IBM's reaction to the
computer is a useful measure of office appliance companies' response
to the new technology. But also because of size, one could expect and
find various points of view within the firm with resulting disagree-
ments about how to deal with computers. The "political" landscape
immediately after World War II (insofar as it affected the computer) in
the company consisted of four general constituencies, two in marketing
and two in manufacturing/development. First was the highly respected
sales force, who had grown up with punched-card machines and knew
nothing of computers. When this new technology became available,
they proved reluctant initially to sell it. Allied with the sales force to a
large extent for many years were executives in New York who, too,

had grown up with tabulating equipment. Although pockets of computer proponents existed in the early 1950s at "corporate" (e.g., in the Product Planning Department), they constantly faced considerable resistance to new ideas until those ideas were fully and frequently justified.[43]

Manufacturing and, especially, engineering made up the other two constituencies. The laboratory and manufacturing teams at Endicott, the Mecca of punched-card equipment, jealously and effectively defended its technology throughout the 1940s and 1950s while dabbling in early computer projects. The IBM manager responsible for proposing R&D budgets in the late 1950s commented how as late as the end of the decade, when it was becoming increasingly obvious that the days of the punched card were rapidly ending, punched-card proponents could still marshall sufficient power to have research funds assigned to this line of business.[44] The fourth group consisted of development engineers at the Poughkeepsie laboratory who, in the minds of the first three constituencies, frequently worked on much leading-edge R&D in the late 1940s and early 1950s. It was into this facility that so many new electrical engineers were hired in the period and to which technical leadership came. They made most of IBM's computer products possible and could count on frequent support from Thomas Watson, Jr. In fact, every computer developed by IBM in the 1950s either came from Poughkeepsie or was influenced by its engineers. This constituency has been the most studied by eloquent members,[45] and its opinions have been most frequently cited in court cases about IBM's early role in the computer business.[46]

Thus, the political landscape in the 1940s and early 1950s was structured in such a way that the move to computers was painful because it was bucking the established norm. The ability of the company to get behind the computer and, finally, to support it by the mid to late 1950s, however, made IBM very successful for years to come. The conversion represented an example of the firm's discipline and commitment, which contrasted with that of most of its rivals, who could not marshall the focus or resources needed to counter IBM. More than thirty years after the initial battles between IBM and Remington Rand for the computer market began, Thomas Watson, Jr., commented on the issue of focus. In response to a question about Remington Rand he said that IBM "knocked [it] out of the park because they built profits by looking at balance sheets. Father built profits by studying tangible assets and he never was distracted by the greed of diversification—no razors for us! We kept our heads down and focused solely on the manipulation of numbers, words, and later, images."[47] The enthusiastic, concentrated support for computers in the late 1950s has drawn much applause from students of the industry. That degree of commitment of emotion, resources, and funding earlier had made the company successful with punched-card equipment. As with punched-card technology, commitment to a major line of business was not free of corporate political or legitimate business concerns. But once made, the same committed energy effectively implemented a successful new course.

IBM's engineering community replaced tabulating products with more sophisticated calculators, using advanced electronics that emerged out of World War II primarily for scientific and military applications. From that change IBM moved toward development of computers. The SSEC (introduced in 1948) had stored-program capability. IBM's Applied Science Group, responsible for advanced electronics in the late 1940s, however, did not become heavily involved with computers until the Korean War. IBM managers called on various U.S. government agencies in 1950 to obtain funding for computer-related projects.[48] One result was the Defense Calculator, later known as the IBM 701. That machine, introduced in 1952, was the first computer of which multiple copies were manufactured; prior machines of that sophistication had been built one at a time. IBM's James Birkenstock described it at the time as an "Electronic Data Processing Machine," creating the term EDP, which was so widely used to describe computers in the next two decades.

Engineers at Poughkeepsie pushed for a smaller device, rekindling their campaign in the fall of 1952. Tremendous resistance to the proposal came from marketing, as with the 701. Marketing managers in New York expressed concern over who would buy or rent the machine. Yet Tom Watson, Jr., approved its construction, and in 1953 the IBM 650 was announced as a general-purpose commercial computer. First shipped in 1954, the 650 proved a successful product with some eighteen hundred copies manufactured, far exceeding all forecasts for demand. No other computer had been manufactured in such quantities.

The success of this computer, more than that of any other in that period, finally caused IBM's key executives to recognize the value of computers in the commercial world of data processing. IBM 650s were sold not just to scientific and government customers. Many were acquired by commercial establishments for inventory control (as at Caterpillar Tractor) and manufacturing processing (e.g., by Chrysler). The 650 system was inexpensive, reliable, and relatively easy to use.[49] The IBM 702 (a member of a series of computers in a family called the 700 systems) came out in 1953; fourteen were installed in the middle of the decade.

Many in IBM's engineering community, both in Endicott and Poughkeepsie, had become increasingly vocal in calling for the construction of computer products by 1950–51. Despite problems with the sales and marketing organizations, they began conversations with potential customers to determine requirements for new machines, from which information they built business cases that made possible many of the early commercial computer projects.[50] In this manner computer proponents convinced the market-driven senior management, particularly Tom Watson, Jr., to approve construction of the IBM 650 (built at Endicott). Years later, engineers at IBM concurred that demand for computers created by the Korean War was a real breakthrough for advocates of the new technology because perceived need for computers together with government demand sufficiently convinced Watson and other executives to support increased, substantial R&D in computers beyond that supported by government contracts.[51]

In fact, work done during the Korean War had a fundamental influence on the engineering community and, later, on the marketing organization at IBM. Engineers later wrote:

> The 701 experience was uniquely important in the history of IBM's transition from punched-card machines to electronic computers. Before that experience, planning and marketing executives could speculate endlessly on whether data could safely be entrusted to invisible tape recording or control entrusted to the ethereal stored program. But when it had been demonstrated that 701s could be manufactured, programmed, maintained, and relied upon for useful results as promised, the speculation subsided. The question thereafter was not whether to build new computers but which machines to introduce and when; and by March 1955 when the nineteenth 701 was installed, the company had announced a variety of new computers.[52]

Two other projects of the period also influenced IBM's thinking within the engineering community: the SAGE and Whirlwind applications. SAGE was one of the largest computer-based applications undertaken in the 1950s to provide an air-defense system for the United

States. It involved dozens of corporations, millions of dollars, and development of new hardware and software throughout the 1950s. Whirlwind, a computer system under development at MIT, also involved many subcontractors and was merged with the SAGE project. Whirlwind was the first real-time control computer. IBM was responsible for building the computers used in SAGE and, obviously, was exposed to design issues for both projects.[53]

Success with these various projects reinforced the attitude expressed by engineers regarding the 700 series. The 650 surprised its designers with its acceptance in the market.[54] SAGE and Whirlwind were the kinds of learning experiences made easier to afford by government funding. In sum, by the mid-1950s a major shift was taking place within the engineering community at IBM, as Poughkeepsie's influence increasingly rose while that of Endicott's punched-card proponents slowly declined in the late 1950s.

One of the fundamental characteristics of IBM's computer-building activities of the 1950s was its ability to move from fabricating one-of-a-kind or a few machines to many computers. That achievement made it possible to produce hundreds of machines within a reasonable period and to control costs and, hence, pricing and profits. Still awaiting its historian is the story of how IBM was able to accomplish what was, for the nascent computer business, a feat. A couple of obvious elements were at work. Additional taxes on profits during the Korean War created an incentive for all businesses to reinvest earnings back into the business. IBM, like all other major manufacturing companies in the office appliance industry, plowed profits back into plant modernization projects rather than pay extra taxes. During the Korean War IBM's plants were retooled, and the facilities at Poughkeepsie and Endicott were modified to handle the manufacture of more complicated electronically based machines. IBM understood how to manufacture precision equipment for both the military and for its punched-card business and simply applied the same principles to the fabrication of computers. Increasingly during the 1950s, standard circuits and packaging became the norm, particularly by the late 1950s. From the earliest days of the 1950s IBM focused on automation of fabrication. As early as when it had to build ferrite-core memories for Whirlwind, it did so with high-speed core-pressing machinery, a process much like making pills.

Each success built on the previous ones so that by the end of the decade the expectation was that all computers would be manufactured in quantity and that design of such devices would take into account manufacturing efficiencies.[55]

Outside the manufacturing arena and despite the push toward computers evident in, say, Poughkeepsie, it was a slow trip in the early years in the market. In 1954, for example, American customers took delivery on some nineteen 701s along with nearly two dozen Remington Rand UNIVACs. The number of computers was still so low that R&D expenses forced high rentals in comparison with lower rentals for mass-produced machines such as the older IBM 604s of which more than two thousand were already installed. Calculators, in short, were still more cost-effective. Both the trade press and IBM's sales force questioned the 702's relevance for that reason and, perhaps, out of ignorance of possible new applications. What became clear at that time, however, was that if the company were to effectively sell computers to match computers to applications, its technology costs had to drop, reliability rise, and manufacturing personnel become adept at mass production.

One by-product of IBM's mid-decade computer projects was the company's commitment to Project STRETCH, to "take a giant step" forward. STRETCH was funded by government sources and conceived by IBM. The firm intended for STRETCH to generate technological innovations that, by early 1961, would allow the firm to ship new computers to customers. The project drew a lot of controversy within IBM and later among historians and veterans of the project. At the time, many executives (including Watson) considered STRETCH a relative failure because of the many technical problems encountered.[56] Years later, after the announcement and success of the IBM S/360 family of computers, which employed many technical features first developed in the STRETCH program, company management acknowledged its learning benefits and its accomplishments.[57]

STRETCH began as another government-funded project in 1955 to build a computer named the 7030 for the Los Alamos Scientific Laboratory. Substantial increases in capacity and speed were anticipated, and in the end it turned out to be IBM's first "supercomputer." Eight were built in the late 1950s. Crucial to IBM's future was that it built on the strategy of packaging components to ease manufacturing. Successes in this area were achieved for components, such as transistors, magnetic core storage, and circuitry. It merged desire to build transistor-based computers with the lessons learned while working on SAGE,

Whirlwind, and real-time systems in the early to mid-1950s. It was a leap forward from vacuum tube technology to transistors, heralding a second generation of computers for the firm with unknown costs, manufacturing problems, and pricing risks. Computer architecture had to be rethought along with the functions of computers in general. The big disappointment was that it cost millions of dollars more than projected, which the company had to absorb. The $40.7 million overrun irritated senior executives, whereas engineers were frustrated because they could not quantify benefits that they knew would accrue from the new processes and technologies developed for these machines.[58]

One of the most important benefits to come from the project was an understanding of how to develop what became known as standard modular systems (SMS) component packaging. SMS became the basis of second-generation computer architecture at IBM. Back panel wiring and circuit card manufacturing became better understood, building on skills acquired on previous projects of the early 1950s. These lessons were applied across all IBM's computer products of the late 1950s and early 1960s and gave courage to those who had to worry about large manufacturing orders anticipated for the S/360 computers of the mid-1960s. The project remains a marvel of technological improvements in the evolution of computers despite the fact that it was scrubbed because of enormous cost overruns.[59] As with all major projects in the office appliance industry, no technology was allowed to advance unless the U.S. government was prepared to pay for the full costs of development or the project was profitable. The technical merits of the technology simply were of secondary importance.

The series of steps taken by engineering management to acquire knowledge of electronics during World War II, implementation of such information in advanced calculating machines, and development of both the business case for computers and actual machines in the early to late 1950s gave IBM the opportunity to enter the computer business. Along the way, initial resistance came from the marketing side of the house and from tabulating machine proponents within engineering. In hindsight, the concern expressed by marketing made sense in a market-driven, profit-oriented enterprise such as IBM or even Remington Rand. The evidence from Burroughs suggests a similar course of action.

Potential is an important issue for those proposing new applications of technology, particularly when it includes high or unknown cost risks. The initial concept of the potential of the computer was not positive, obviously driven as much by ignorance of the technology as by any other issue. One marketing employee of the period recalled that "99 percent of the IBM data processing sales force knew nothing" about computers.[60] Those who did thought of the CPC in the late 1940s, for example, as a niche product for scientists and government customers. The same held true for the 701. The sales force did not yet appreciate the impact the 650 would have: "Few of us in the field felt the winds of change blowing in the summer of 1953."[61] Marketing executives at corporate headquarters supported the 650 only when it became obvious that they needed to respond to the seven vendors selling computers against the older CPCs, who had attacked the market for the IBM 604. This was a very narrow response to a perceived limited market demand. In 1954, with fits and starts still a problem with computers, IBM announced the 701 scientific computer. Marketing representatives and their managers initially reacted negatively, balking at the $20,000 per month rental, which put the machine out of reach of most customers. At the time many sales people were still concerned about whether they could even place the 650, which rented for one-sixth the cost of a 701 and was more card-oriented.[62]

The problem faced by marketing within IBM was cost. The smallest stored-program computers of the early 1950s were more expensive than punched-card configurations. The 650, which for a minimum configuration rented for $3,250 per month during the mid-1950s, was equal in cost to two Type 402 or 407 accounting machines, two reproducers, two sorters, one collator, one electromechanical multiplying punch, and six keypunches and verifiers. Many small customers, therefore, had no use for such a machine. Larger companies faced the problem of converting old practices, forms, and so forth, to new ones in order to use a computer.[63]

It took the 650's proponents seven years from the time they conceptualized the need for a small computer until it appeared. If one were to pick the event that led to its acceptance at IBM headquarters, it was the installation of a UNIVAC I at the U.S. Bureau of the Census, which emotionally charged Watson and others near him to consider a response, although it was not clear at the time exactly what the reaction should be.[64] During 1953 and 1954 development of the 702 was poor, beset with engineering problems, which simply raised more questions about the practicality of such a product. Watson personally had to intervene to ensure effective resolution of technical problems. Meanwhile, as Simmons noted in his memoirs, the marketing community at headquarters still believed that punched-card equipment would remain the staple of the company for years to come. Marketing representatives and service personnel in the field lacked facts about how to use and maintain the 702; customers did not receive adequate instruction on how to take advantage of its capabilities, and technical literature proved unclear and scarcely usable.[65]

At divisional and corporate levels, R&D continued to be dominated by punched-card partisans. Simmons, then manager of Product Planning, found the Endicott community politically well in charge of R&D budgets. It received the lion's share of R&D funds in the mid-1950s, which at the time approached 2 percent of IBM's total gross income.[66] Even STRETCH could not shake loose the commitment to punched-card technology and was created as a reaction to Remington Rand as much as a way to enhance electronics at IBM.

Yet, beginning in the period 1953–54, belief grew within the company that change had to come. The large installed base of IBM punched-card equipment, most of which had already been fully depreciated and accounted for more than 90 percent of all such machines installed in the United States, was only invulnerable within that market, and the only serious rivals were Remington Rand, NCR, and, potentially, Burroughs. The growing concern was the threat looming on the horizon from the computer with numerous vendors entering or announcing their intent to enter the market, and it was during the period 1954–57 that marketing executives at IBM finally made the conversion to a procomputer position. They then increasingly worried about how to market new computer products in the late 1950s to gain a leading position in the new market while not compromising the cash cow of punched-card equipment. As IBM's revenues from electronic data-processing (EDP) equipment increased, the easier it became for marketing executives to endorse the new technology. As they read their copies of the 1956 annual report in early 1957, they would have learned that in the previous year IBM had obtained 14 percent of its $892 million in revenues from computer products.[67]

IBM's product-planning manager, who had most strongly endorsed computers throughout the 1950s, complained that in 1958 he was still finding resistance to the computer within IBM.[68] That year Simmons reported that he had proposed an R&D budget that slashed support for punched-card equipment and shifted all the funds to computer development because he thought the days of punched-card technology were numbered. He presented his budget, as he did each year, to Watson, who reacted by saying: "Simmons, you're wrong. Wrong. WRONG! WRONG! Can't you understand? You're WRONG!"[69] In the room were IBM's top marketing executives; none came to his defense. Were they hostile or simply prudent politically in not daring to challenge the head of IBM? Regardless of their thoughts or actions that day Simmons believed that "by seeming to denigrate the heart-and-soul of IBM, the product line that paid the bills and made stock options possible for middle managers like me, I had shot myself in the foot."[70]

The situation changed, but more slowly than he wanted. The financial community within IBM worried about profits and, therefore, was very reluctant to abandon punched-card sales. Not until 1962 did income from computers exceed that from punched-card equipment. One group of engineers later recalled that it was not until IBM sold copies of its 1401 computer system (announced in October 1959 and shipped in quantity in 1960) to small- and medium-sized customers that many in the firm finally got their "first realistic glimpse of the size and importance of the computer market that was unfolding."[71]

Watson presented his view of how he and his company approached the computer opportunity in his memoirs. During the early 1950s he had encouraged and supported the study of computer technology and, more specifically, electronics. By the mid-1950s, however, he recalled that "demand for those products was accelerating, and it seemed clear the market wasn't going to wait. If IBM didn't grab the business, somebody else would, and we would never have this kind of opportunity again."[72] But he moved into the market with caution. Watson recognized that one of his great assets was the IBM sales force, but it had to be retrained and partially replaced in the late 1950s and early 1960s with members capable of selling computers. In hindsight, "technology turned out to be less important than sales and distribution methods. Starting with UNIVAC, we consistently outsold people who had better technology because we knew how to put the story before the customers, how to install the machines successfully, and how to hang on to the customers once we had them."[73] As early as 1956, he had begun to see this change in market conditions rushing in on him; yet IBM was showing excellent results: "By the time the presidential election rolled around in 1956, we had eighty-seven machines in operation and one hundred-ninety on order, against forty-one in operation and forty on order for all other computer-makers."[74]

But those volumes could not totally displace tabulator revenues in the late–1950s. That reality caused him to balk at Simmons's suggestion that the company rush quickly away from tabulating machines toward the computer. Pacing the timing of the change was as important to Watson as the change itself—a classic marketing issue throughout the history of office appliances and, later, information processing.

The view just presented of how IBM reacted to the creation of the computer contrasts with earlier accounts in several respects. Unlike in most previous interpretations, one sees a company that first and foremost reacted to market conditions. The charge was always led by marketing considerations; financial managers provided ammunition. It was also a company made up of diverse groups with various opinions about the computer competing for R&D funding and political support. On the one hand, IBM was a company pondering the merits of the computer from the earliest days of that technology's history and investing substantially in its base technologies by 1950. On the other hand, it was a firm whose senior executives refused to introduce computer products until they felt they had to (because of customer demands or competitors) or they could see a return on their investment (as in providing the military with machines during the Korean War, which led to modernized manufacturing plants).[75]

The largest, undefined risk to revenue, of course, was the possibility that computers would displace tabulating equipment. The company understood very well from decades of experience that introducing innovations always cannibalized, to some extent, existing sources of revenues. As the evidence from Watson suggests, moving slowly to new introductions made economic good sense, especially with a company such as IBM, which had the dominant position in an existing market. Thus, the conservatism portrayed in my account of IBM's actions is a response to the threat that innovation posed.

Emerging clearly is a picture of a company that is very effective in making profitable and reliable equipment but not as fully committed to computer products as previous writers on the industry believed. Once involved fully, however, it sold many useful machines. In short, IBM worked both sides of the street well, selling punched-card equipment for as long as it made sense while making a growing and then total commitment to lead the computer market. IBM proved reluctant to give up a more than forty-year heritage in punched-card equipment until the late 1950s, and then only prudently. It was no accident, therefore, that IBM made its famous "bet your company" decision to build the S/360 family of computers in 1961 rather than several years earlier and only when it had to survive against growing competition.

The Role of Remington Rand

Remington Rand emerged from World War II with a large, diversified collection of businesses catering to both office appliance markets and to defense. Like IBM, it had acquired additional skills in electronics. But its strategy for acquiring computer-based technology was different from IBM's, as was its response to the machines. In large part, Remington Rand's reaction to computers was no surprise; it reflected a continuation of a strategy evident from its birth and management throughout the 1930s and 1940s. Unlike IBM, which by the end of World War II had been a relatively integrated organization for more than fifteen years, Remington Rand consisted of a number of different entities merged loosely and run by an aging James H. Rand (1886–1968), who had little appreciation of the new electronics. Rand had not been able fully to integrate marketing, manufacturing, or R&D by the end of World War II. Top management continued to allow sections of the company to vie for attention and to compete for resources, people, and research. The same problem appeared later at GE and at RCA, and again even in the 1980s and 1990s at Unisys (the successor to Burroughs after Burroughs merged with Sperry, which contained part of the old Remington Rand).

When the company identified a new line of business with sufficient opportunity to pursue, it realistically had one of two options. First, it could assign the opportunity to an existing division. That strategy was appropriate if the new market was sufficiently large to be supported appropriately by the designated division (e.g., the development of electrical typewriters). Second, the parent company could acquire a company already established in the new line of business, preferably one in financial trouble, which would ensure a good deal. The second approach represented the company's initial response to computers. Management saw the potential for computer sales perhaps more clearly than did most companies in the 1940s. They recognized that the fastest way to enter that market was by acquiring companies already in the field that had potential products to sell and the technical staff to develop them. Remington Rand believed it could sell such products. This was a strategy adopted much later also by NCR and Burroughs. In hindsight, poor marketing and management of R&D contributed to Remington Rand's inability to stay on top as the leader in this market. Yet the company believed that two characteristics—a product and a technical staff—were absolutely essential if the firm were to enter the fledgling computer business quickly at low risk.[76]

When historians compare and contrast the responses of IBM and Remington Rand to the computer business, they quickly and correctly point out that the reason IBM did better in that market by the late 1950s was its total commitment to the new line.[77] There is little doubt about that fact although it was not necessarily obvious to managers in various computer, electronics, and office appliance firms in the early 1950s how extensive their commitment of R&D had to be to compete successfully in the computer business. That realization began unfolding in the mid-1950s and had become very obvious by the early 1960s.[78]

The strategies employed by these two companies call out their fundamental differences and go far to explain why IBM did make the commitment necessary to be so successful in the new industry. For IBM the issue of entering the computer business was increasingly central to its existence because it was fairly clear to a growing number of key managers by the early to mid-1950s that such technology had the potential to displace the company's main line of business. That conversion, and how it was done, was as much a "bet your company" series of decisions as that to build the S/360 in the 1960s.[79] The main difference in strategy lay in that the first (as taken by Remington Rand and Burroughs) was a series of steps taken one by one in reaction to immediate conditions, whereas the second (the IBM approach) represented a dramatic, single decision with full knowledge of the strategic intent involved. The decisions made in the early 1950s were accompanied by anguish over time; nonetheless, they reflected the company's one-line-of-business circumstance.

Remington Rand approached the computer as simply another business line to add to its collection. To be sure, the computer could also displace the old Powers tabulating equipment (or be displaced by other computer vendors), but because that portion of the business did not constitute the bulk of the product line, the risk to Remington Rand was less than that to IBM. The real issue for senior management at Remington Rand was whether or not to get into a new line of business while maintaining all the old ones. By acquiring two computer-based companies, the company in effect answered the question by adding, not displacing, a line of business. That strategy proved weak, however, because once initiated, computer R&D had to compete for funds and people—first, between the two computer pieces of the business, and, second, among all divisions of the company. Although competition in R&D is not in itself bad, because it can be productive, it does present the real possibility of duplication in products caused by R&D investments. Duplication of product lines is worrisome because it always leads to inefficiency and is a waste of resources. IBM did not face that problem in the 1950s; it did, however, by the mid-1970s.

When what it would take to be successful in the computer business became obvious, it was too late for Remington Rand. It had spread itself too thinly across not only its own two computer businesses but over the entire company. By the late 1950s IBM had little choice but to dig deeper into the world of computers. Add to that circumstance, therefore, IBM's more rapid product introduction pace, its more efficient manufacturing skills in information-processing equipment, and, ultimately, a better motivated and trained sales force armed with an effective corporate marketing strategy, and it becomes understandable why management at IBM could compete with and then surpass Remington Rand's management in the budding world of computer sales.[80] Remington Rand's diversity of opportunities combined with its nonintegrated organization and poor marketing skills to hamper its effectiveness in the late 1940s and throughout the 1950s as it had in the 1930s.

Although IBM found it very painful to enter the computer world after World War II, Remington Rand found it less so because of its diversity and acquisitive strategy. Thus, in the early 1950s James Rand could make the initial and highly visible splash into the new business simply by acquiring two companies that were developing electronic digital computers. He acquired the Eckert-Mauchly Computer Corporation in Philadelphia in 1950 and two years later Engineering Research Associates (ERA) of St. Paul. Eckert and Mauchly had been two of the key engineers on the ENIAC project at the Moore School of Electrical Engineering. After their dispute over patent rights to that and other computer-based projects, they left the University of Pennsylvania and established their firm, in the words of Eckert, to "build a very

small machine that could be used in a chemical plant or power station
. . . to control some simple problems they had there."[81] They called
their company Electronic Controls but found they could not produce
the device intended and, thus, changed the name of the firm and built
what eventually became the UNIVAC. In 1948 they signed a contract
with the Bureau of Standards to construct the BINAC, the sequel to the
ENIAC and the EDVAC, and one year later constructed the BINAC
(1949) for Northrop Aviation.

These two engineers envisioned the UNIVAC as the first commercially available general-purpose electronic digital computer.[82] At the
time Remington Rand acquired the firm (1950), the machine was under
construction. The first UNIVAC was delivered in 1951 to the Bureau
of the Census at a price of approximately $1 million.[83] To develop this
machine they modified existing electronic components to configure the
new system. The cost of development was so high that the two engineers eventually had to seek a company like Remington Rand to acquire them, fund their project until completion, and help place the six
to twelve machines they thought could be sold. In 1954 the first commercial use of a UNIVAC came with GE's installation of one at its
appliance manufacturing plant in Louisville, Kentucky. That event
brought sufficient attention to the machine to help Remington Rand
sell some forty copies, even making the word *univac* synonymous with
the word *computer* for a few years.[84] Thus, the Eckert-Mauchly Computer Corporation acquisition clearly and quickly thrust an unprepared
Remington Rand into the midst of a new business.

Remington Rand then consummated its second purchase. ERA had
been formed in 1946 by former naval officers who had been led by
U.S. Navy officials to believe that they could count on government
contracts for communications and computer-based products in the
postwar period.[85] Like the Eckert-Mauchly enterprise, ERA proved
effective in building a machine. As noted previously, ERA made the
Atlas I (1950). ERA obtained permission from the U.S. government to
seek commercial customers for modified versions of the Atlas. The
commercial product, called the 1101 and initially shipped in December
1950, appeared before the first UNIVAC left its own laboratory. The
1102 was introduced in 1952; three of each machine ultimately were
sold.[86] By the time Remington Rand had acquired the company,
ERA's engineers were already developing the 1103. They began de-
liveries in 1953, eventually selling twenty. ERA had some five hun-

dred employees, making it a sizable operation and, perhaps, the largest in the world dedicated to the construction of commercial computers. According to ERA sources, it had shipped about "80 percent of the value of electronic computers in existence in the United States" by the end of 1952; for the moment that placed Remington Rand at the head of the new computer business.[87]

Remington Rand (renamed Sperry Rand Corporation after another merger in 1955), however, faced difficulties very quickly. William Norris, one of the founders of ERA, later testified that Remington Rand failed to make the kind of "financial commitment that was necessary," let alone pay sufficient attention to the computer business. Product development came too slowly.[88] As noted, the UNIVAC II was introduced in 1957, by which time IBM (which still drew most of its revenues from punched-card equipment) had introduced many computer-based products that sold in much larger volumes than anything coming out of its old rival. Henry Forrest, also from ERA, later commented that Remington Rand "did not mount an adequate sales effort, and did not choose to create the kind of organization that [had] all the parts such as support people, [and] the manufacturing facilities to meet the market that then existed."[89] Similar complaints came from the Eckert-Mauchly group. Mauchly wrote in 1954, "Remington Rand has not been willing to pay sufficient expenditure for any phase of the electronic computer sales program."[90] Its sales people were not compensated for selling UNIVAC, only tabulating equipment.

IBM's sales representatives received commissions for selling either one. No investment was made by Remington Rand to educate its sales staff about computers, whereas at IBM an effort was mounted in the 1950s to do just that.[91] Mauchly could see the difference from his own perch: "The IBM Company was doing what I would call an aggressive job, both in marketing and in development of the things to market, and I felt that the Remington Rand Company was losing a position which was in their favor by being unwilling to do some of the things which seemed obvious."[92]

Slow product introductions and lack of adequate training of either its sales personnel or potential customers led to the predictable loss of key managers at Remington Rand.[93] William Norris, for example, left in 1957 to form the highly successful Control Data Corporation (CDC), taking others with him.[94] Norris, like Eckert and Mauchly, also had been frustrated by rivalry of the two computer groups within the company: "I left Sperry-Rand because of turmoil. This turmoil was made up of confusion, indecision, conflicting orders, organization line breaches, constant organizational change, fighting and unbridled competition between divisions."[95] Another employee noted that the firm had computer development laboratories in Norwalk, Philadelphia, and St. Paul "all attempting essentially, to pursue the same markets and develop similar products. . . . And throughout the years 1953, 1954 and part of 1955 the whole activity with respect to computing in Remington Rand was extremely uncoordinated."[96] In short, as *Business Week* was later to conclude, the company had "snatched defeat from the jaws of victory."[97]

It would be fun to suppose what might have happened internally within IBM had it known to what extent Sperry Rand was confused in the mid-1950s. Probably its only intelligence was that of the marketplace, who was delivering which computers in what quantities; everything else was rumors. Would the company have committed itself sooner and more fully to computers had it known? Perhaps not; tabulating machines still reigned supreme, and the financial fraternity in IBM worried more about current profits than future markets. What helped IBM in the late 1950s, however, was Sperry Rand's lost lead. Ironically, only those within Remington's computer engineering community appreciated the consequences.

Commercial Response in Europe

Given the interest in computing that had existed in Western Europe and, in particular, in Great Britain during the 1930s and throughout World War II, one might have expected Europeans to respond to the commercial use of computers much as did people in the United States and in roughly the same period. They did not. The experienced British, with two decades of research on computers and leading in certain aspects of its technology (e.g., the Williams tube and other forms of memory), were not able to transfer their knowledge from laboratory to market with any speed or effect similar to that in the United States. In all probability this can be accounted for because of the smaller size of national markets and weaker economies in Europe in the late 1940s and early 1950s. While in America commercial computers began to appear in profitable quantities by the late 1950s with more than a dozen firms either participating or considering entering the new field,

British activity remained strikingly limited.[98] A similar tale could be told about activities in Germany, France, or Italy. No commercial systems are known to have been under development, let alone in production, in Eastern Europe or in the Soviet Union, only experimental devices.[99]

Research on the initial development and marketing of commercial computers in Europe has not been done to any meaningful degree, but the situation is beginning to change.[100] From what little was done, several environmental conditions influenced Europe's commercial response to the computer. The economies of leading Western European nations were devastated in the years immediately after World War II, whereas that of the United States proved the healthiest in the world. It took the announcement of the Marshall Plan late in 1947 and its subsequent successful implementation to move Europe from war's destruction to prosperity. That recovery required the total reconstruction of Europe's manufacturing and agricultural capabilities and the reestablishment of distribution and transportation infrastructures. After Marshall Plan aid came to Europe, recovery advanced rapidly in the period from 1948 through the early to mid-1950s.[101] With recovery, demand for information-processing equipment rose; therefore, one could document the demand for office equipment rising after 1948, whereas in the United States, with its intact economy, demand expanded sharply in 1945, and the requirement for computers came earlier. By the time computers were needed in Europe, Europeans were living in the 1950s. Therefore, how Europeans viewed computing may well have been a function of the lag in time between when the technology was developed and when it could have been commercially practical.[102]

The element of timing of technology's migration from laboratory to market was affected because office appliance companies in the United States were able to develop and sell commercial systems earlier than Europeans. Not devastated by war, for example, were Remington Rand and IBM, despite loss of wartime business in Europe, destruction of some manufacturing facilities, and lack of raw materials and energy. So when they began manufacturing computers and other office equipment, they sold these in European markets before indigenous competitors could offer real competition. Marketing through their reestablished European branch offices in the 1950s, Americans captured a large enough share of the market that much of the subsequent history of computing in Western Europe became a reaction to the American presence in the form of nurturing national companies.[103] Even in Great Britain, where an active computer market did develop in the late 1950s dominated by local manufacturers, by the end of 1962, 37 percent of all installed machines were American and by the end of 1965, more than half were; that overwhelming percentage remained constant into the 1970s and machines continued to be sold by office appliance vendors into the late 1960s.[104] In France, American computers were readily available in the 1950s although that situation began to change during the 1960s as local vendors became more effective.[105]

These two environmental factors are directly related to demand for computing. They had to emerge from healthy economies and from those positioned to deliver products sooner or, at least, on a timely basis. These economic considerations should not be confused, however, with activities that did take place, particularly in Great Britain, where individuals and firms were eager to enter the computer market at the same time as others were in the United States. Although the data-processing industry in Britain contrasts markedly with that of the United States (e.g., their respective sizes and effectiveness were very different), it, nonetheless, was active.[106]

In Britain technical knowledge of computers in the 1950s often matched that of the United States, particularly early in the decade. Yet in Great Britain and throughout Europe substantial government support for computer research was absent. That lack of help contrasted sharply to the proactive role played by various agencies of the U.S. government in the postwar period. Shared technical information among engineers in the 1940s, however, made up part of the slack and was one reason why computer scientists came to America to attend lectures at the Moore School and at Harvard from 1946 to 1950. That circumstance changed gradually in the 1950s as commercial enterprises or the need for military secrecy once again slowed the published flow of technological information across international boundaries, but it did not stop it. Meanwhile, in Great Britain as elsewhere, demand for computers was far less, perhaps, because of economic conditions (such as size of a national economy or vitality). Europeans faced another problem: R&D costs, because they are relatively fixed, had to be amortized over all sales. But the European market was too small to make R&D cost per unit low enough to remain competitive with U.S. vendors. Demand suggests the differences of size and volume. For example, in 1955 some 240 computers were installed in the United States,

13 in Britain, 5 each in France and Germany, and none known in Japan.[107] Flamm estimated that in 1960 U.S. firms dominated 100 percent of all computer installations in the United States, 17 percent in Britain, 49 percent in France, 70 percent in Germany, and 56 percent in Japan. Already noted was the growth of the U.S. market share in Britain during the 1960s.[108]

Although various computer projects were under way in British laboratories at the University of Cambridge, Manchester University, and the National Physical Laboratory, the first commercial machine was the Ferranti Mark I, shipped initially in 1951; nine were ultimately sold. The number was small, but so was user interest owing to, as one historian put it, "the inertia of the customers."[109] J. Lyons Company, a food catering firm, contracted with the University of Cambridge for a copy of the EDSAC for its own internal use, which it then marketed as the Leo (Lyons Electronic Office) in the late 1950s.[110] The thought of a food company marketing computers may seem odd to those used to reading of electronics or office supply firms selling computers, but this case may be symptomatic of the environment in which there appeared to be less connection between British universities and British military organizations for support of commercial ventures than in the United States of the early 1950s.

Thus, the model of ERA in the U.S., with military machines being modified for a commercial market, was not replicated in Britain during the 1950s. The few devices constructed (e.g., the J. Lyons processor) were technologically not advanced. The Leo II, first shipped in 1957, was built with vacuum tubes. The British Tabulating Machine Company (BTM), broken off from IBM licensing relations in 1949, sought its technology from one individual, at first Professor Andrew Booth of London University at a time when IBM was hiring dozens of engineers to explore computing electronics in Poughkeepsie. The Powers-Samas organization, also operating in Great Britain, like BTM, lacked advanced technology.[111] In the 1950s in Britain, producers such as Ferranti, Elliott, and English Electric sold machines primarily to scientific users and to the military at a time when American vendors were doing the same but also expanding into a commercial market, particularly in the late 1950s.

The situation in France was also one of delayed response to commercial systems. Although scientific interest in computing in France dated back to the interwar period (e.g., the work of Louis Couffingnal), the effectiveness of technological developments did not approach Great Britain's in either the 1930s or 1940s. Machines Bull, like BTM or IBM, had been an important prewar office appliance firm, but, like its European competitors, it lacked technology or strong ties to university researchers. It paid attention to computer developments by way of its own engineering community and built an experimental machine in 1951 called Gamma 2. It was a calculator, however, and it was not until 1958 that Machines Bull brought out its first electronic digital computer, a machine based on dated technology. Thus, Bull followed both the pattern and timing of British introductions.[112] Another, yet smaller firm, Société d'Electronique et d'Automatisme (SEA), was analogous to the American ERA in that it was a high-technology-based firm created to build electronic devices for the military and, by the late 1950s, was constructing computers.[113] Yet it, too, produced very few machines. No other significant manufacturers of electronic digital computers existed in France before the 1960s. Machines Bull, however, continued to dominate the small commercial market into the 1960s.

In Germany, Konrad Zuse, who had constructed a series of electro-mechanical and, later, electronic machines since the 1930s called the Z series, represented an early exception to an otherwise empty computer landscape in Germany.[114] The economic disruption caused by the collapse of the Nazi regime, the devastation of war, and U.S. military occupation economic regulations ensured that the remaining years of the 1940s would be focused on survival and not on economic expansion. It was in the 1950s, however, that the West German economy made a sufficiently sharp recovery to generate adequate demand for business computers. German universities initially nurtured small computer projects in the early to mid-1950s. In 1955 Zuse began work on a commercial device with the support of Siemens and Standard Elektrik Lorenz. Standard Elektrik introduced its first computers in 1959, Siemens in 1960, and Telefunken A. G. in 1961. Meanwhile, IBM had been manufacturing the IBM 650 in Stuttgart, Germany, since 1956, making that firm the dominant supplier of products in Germany in the late 1950s.[115] Zuse brought out his first commercial machine in 1958 but installed only a few and ultimately sold his company in 1964 to the Swiss industrial conglomerate, Brown Bovieri Mannheim. The Swiss sold the Zuse business within months to Siemens.[116] Thus, in West Germany, as in France, commercial computers were part of the history of the 1960s, not of the 1950s. Obvious, also, was the lack of significant government support in the early years, especially when compared to the experience in the United States.

Although the history of computer developments in other European countries remains almost nonexistent and is just now being investigated, especially in Italy and Scandinavia,[117] the numbers of machines built and sold were tracked by various government agencies and commercial entities. Based on this evidence one can conclude that the computer was not a major item in the economies of any of these countries before the 1960s. Processing information in the 1950s very much depended on punched-card equipment and accounting machines. Commercial computers were built in the late 1950s but on a very limited basis. N. V. Electrologica in the Netherlands, for example, brought out its first machines in 1958, while the giant electrical company, Philips, only flirted with the technology in that decade. Only later did it become a major European supplier.[118] A similar pattern was evident in Italy, Switzerland, and Austria.

One economist looking at the computer industry, primarily in the period after the 1950s, concluded that the Europeans lost the technological and, hence, commercial lead in the early years to the Americans for two reasons: the lack of sufficient government encouragement to develop machines that could be sold commercially, and a base of technical synergy too small to create a European Silicon Valley. Europeans also did not have aggressive military programs to support development of miniaturized electronics as did the United States. Thus, whatever was converted into available commercial products was based on U.S. or British technology. In the 1960s that process changed as European governments began to nurture "national champions."[119] In short, for Europe the age of the computer came at least five years or more later than it had to the United States.

Summary

Office equipment vendors were a wary lot, approaching the new world of computers cautiously. In the United States, in particular, they dabbled in the new technology with federal funding to cover the large cost and risk of expense overruns. Markets were narrowly defined at first—military and scientific applications—but expanded slowly during the early 1950s more in response to customers requesting such products than in a fundamental attempt to create new markets. Evidence of real demand creation would not surface until the late 1950s. These companies did not move into the world of computers gracefully; they worried when competitive pressures and market demand dictated that they provide products. IBM responded best of all, always maximizing its marketing, technical, and economic assets while keeping its focus fully on information handling. Rivals in electronics (such as GE and RCA), communications (e.g., AT&T), computers (Bull in the French economy and ERA or Eckert-Mauchly in the U.S.), diversified office appliance vendors (NCR, Burroughs, and Remington Rand, for instance) were not focused enough to make a success of the new business. With hindsight it is very easy to conclude that they had difficulty making suitable products with which to compete and in gaining customers. It appears also in retrospect that the best opportunity to move from older methods to computerized ones depended from a marketing point of view on the ability of a firm to take customers already dependent on mechanical information processing to newer technologies, in effect, improving upon older methods to do previously defined applications (e.g., payroll and inventory control). Relying on leading-edge customers in science and the military, while it afforded office appliance vendors initial entry into the computer business, in the long run did not generate sales as significant as their commercial accomplishments by the end of the 1960s. Furthermore, as it became increasingly evident how massive the investment to continue R&D (late 1950s to early 1960s) would have to be, sales outside of the military, government, and scientific communities were required to sustain a credible effort.

In contrast to the office appliance vendors was a staggering number of small start-up firms that moved quickly into the American computer business in the 1950s. By any count this number exceeded seventy enterprises. Focusing on military, scientific, and engineering customers, and with no financial stake in the broad office appliance market, they depended largely on the largesse of U.S. government contracts. They usually remained small niche players, always undercapitalized, and consequently few survived intact. Those that made it into the 1960s and beyond did so first as suppliers of scientific and engineering minicomputers, second by continuing to serve government customers, and third by broadening their appeal to commercial buyers.

The circumstance in Europe was more one of timing and size. The devastation of World War II and the fractured European economy with its comparatively small national economies simply delayed the computer's commercial viability. The delay ranged from five to ten years in the West and up to twenty years in the Soviet block. Although many authors have argued that the infusion of R&D dollars from the U.S. government made possible the development and marketing of commercial machines, in the long run economic conditions and incentives were far more influential in establishing and expanding demand for computers around the world. The lag in Europe for computers simply was one example of that fact. The British, for example, had no difficulty transporting U.S.-developed technology between roughly 1945 and 1952, most of which was funded by the U.S. government, and merging it with their own excellent work in the field. If the British had a specific weakness (besides their economy), it was poor marketing.[120] French, German, Dutch, and Soviet engineers could also just as easily subscribe to American journals recording important advances in the period. But it was the ability of organizations, such as IBM and Remington Rand, to deliver products at a time when commercial demand for them ultimately developed that made possible transformation of increasingly reliable equipment from laboratory and special-purpose applications into a generally available set of products.

During the migration from laboratory to market, awareness of the new technology grew as it moved from a small circle of specialists to a wider public and helped to make acceptable the idea that computers could be used efficiently. That raises very important questions: What were readers and potential customers in the United States learning about these machines? How did they respond to the computer? These are the subjects of chapter 5.

5

The Public and Customers
Meet the Computer

How the American public and, subsequently, customers and users of computers responded initially to the new technology is a nearly unknown subject. The same can be said of circumstances in Europe. Yet the questions this topic raises are crucial to any appreciation of how the data-processing industry converted from electromechanical accounting equipment and punched-card gear to computers and, finally, how society became so closely dependent on and identified with the new technology. At best, one can find comments buried sporadically in memoirs of various participants in the industry to the effect that in the beginning people knew nothing of the new equipment and had to learn about it before they could find possible uses. But those are obvious statements that shed little light on what and when Americans were told, where they received their information, and what were the issues and attitudes that emerged from the spread of information on the new technology. An early step toward acceptance was knowing that computers existed, which required moving information about them from laboratories to the general public. Information appeared primarily in the form of publications in widely distributed magazines, particularly industry-specific journals and, then, in advertisements. To a lesser extent, some information was communicated via radio and, later, television. Novels and short stories also created an image, although not as accurate as what otherwise appeared in print. Studying primarily what appeared in journals and newspapers offers a useful insight into what data became available to Americans. One could conclude that awareness was a precondition to acceptance of the new machines because it made people optimistic about the potential benefits of these devices before anybody had to make decisions that led to reliance upon them to do the work of their companies and agencies.

The Public's Knowledge

The dissemination of information at the end of World War II in the United States occurred in several phases. First, those working on war-related projects shared their knowledge with interested fellow scientists. It was no surprise that in the first several years following the war, seminars were held at Harvard University, where the Mark I had been built, and at the University of Pennsylvania, home of the ENIAC. The population of several hundred engineers and scientists interested in computers in the period 1945–48 received the bulk of their information from such sessions. Seminal papers were often mimeographed or published in limited quantities, and also passed through this small circle of interested people, a circle that swelled rapidly during the early 1950s.[1]

Second, more general scientific journals began to publish on the subject at almost the same time (such as *Mathematical Tables and Other Aids to Computing*) and over the next several years increased the volume of their coverage of the new technology. The pattern was one of incremental growth in the number of articles per publication and, later, in the number of publications carrying articles. In 1945, for example, articles appeared in *Science Digest* and in the *Science News Letter*, which were more widely read than the scholarly journals published by, for instance, the American Philosophical Society or by the Association for Computing Machines (ACM), formed in September 1947.[2] In 1946 U.S. articles appeared in *Senior Scholastic, Popular Mechanics, Popular Science, Scientific American,* and *Science Illustrated.*[3] This pattern remained evident over the next several years as the numbers of publications increased, but all were aimed at relatively limited, serious audiences. In 1947 *Popular Science* published two articles, *Scientific American* another, and *Science News Letter* four.[4] These publications described various machines under construction during World War II. As the 1940s passed, the subjects shifted to projects under way after the war. That genre continued to thrive all during the early 1950s; in the late 1950s the shift was to a combination of machine descriptions and, what today one might call application

Table 5.1

Initial Publication Dates of Key U.S. Computer-focused Journals, 1943–60

Journal	Year
Mathematical Tables and Other Aids to Computation	1943–60
Digital Computer Newsletter	1948
Computers and Automation	1951
Association for Computing Machinery Journal	1954
Datamation	1957
IBM Journal of Research and Development	1957
Computer Journal	1958

briefs (in which the uses of such devices were described almost invariably in glowing terms).

For the "computer scientist" (if one dares apply that term before the 1960s!), focused publications increased in number between the 1940s and the 1960s. The initial publication dates for key journals dedicated to computing and read by developers of computers are listed in Table 5.1. As one would reasonably expect, of the seven publications listed, the most widely circulated appeared in the late 1950s, reflecting the growing demand for information on computing.

With the lifting of war-time secrecy, interest in calculators (as computers were known at the time) began to be reflected in the more widely read magazines of the day, such as *Time, Newsweek, Business Week,* and *Collier's.* In 1945 *Newsweek* and *Business Week* each ran an article on calculators; in 1946 these magazines published additional material and were joined by *Time* and *Life.*[5] In 1947 came the first major growth period for such literature: all articles were descriptive and appeared in larger numbers of publications than before. The following year, *Business Week* and *Newsweek* each ran three articles, and additional publications brought out other pieces.[6] These articles reflected the same kind of generally accepted optimism that pervaded the times—that technology was good, efficient, and promised great things for the future.[7]

For the number of articles appearing on the subject of calculators and calculating machines in the United States between the start of 1945 and the close of 1960, as listed in the *Reader's Guide to Periodical Literature* and in the index to the *New York Times,* see Figure 5.1, page 106. These two lists, which did not catalog technical or trade publications and, hence, understated the number of articles on the subject, are useful to view what was being published in widely distributed magazines and journals. Clearly, the number of entries in the *Reader's Guide* suggested that the subject was receiving relatively minor notice until the mid-1950s and then reached a level of publication that remained higher than in the 1940s until the boom period of the 1960s. The decline in citations in Figure 5.1 in the period 1956–58 can be attributed to the fact that by then articles describing computers were becoming old topics. This interpretation was borne out by the simultaneous increase in articles announcing new computer-related events. Interestingly, it was not until 1961 that the *Reader's Guide* established a separate category for articles on Electronic Data Processing. Articles concerning computers were listed under that heading. The change was evident in the handling of the topic by many American publishers of the time.

In Figure 5.1 the trend line for the *New York Times* tracks yet a different set of data. Whereas the kinds of materials generally cataloged in the *Reader's Guide* were descriptions of computers and related projects, articles in the *New York Times* were mostly about events, particularly in the earlier years. For example, pieces would appear when computers were installed at important agencies. By the late 1950s this type of material was augmented with articles describing how they were being used. The *New York Times* trend line in Figure 5.1 suggests when other newspapers, too, might have thought computer-related stories and events newsworthy, that is, of interest to the public. As with the *Reader's Guide,* the evidence implies that computers were not important to large- and medium-sized businesses and their executives until the mid-1950s. One can infer from the data, also, that the public did not receive substantial amounts of information on the new technology until the mid-1950s. Finally, in the index for the *New York Times* the categories under which articles appeared were a barometer of how people cataloged and treated information about computers. In that index computer articles were listed under the heading "Mathematics" until 1948, "Calculators" until 1956, and then "Data Processing Machines."

Although the evidence presented in these two indices bolsters the argument that computers did not begin to play a significant role within the data-processing/office appliance industry until the late 1950s, one can go too far in relying on such information. No work has been done on public perceptions during this period by methodically reviewing in

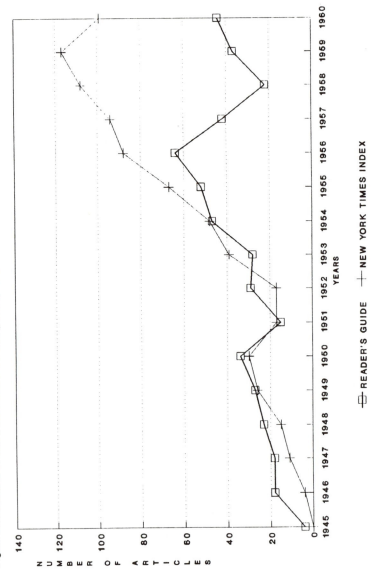

Figure 5.1. **Number of U.S. Publications on Computers, 1945–60**

Sources: Reader's Guide and New York Times Index

detail a wide range of publications. In one fascinating study of computer advertisements a researcher examined more than ten thousand ads that appeared from 1950 to 1980[8] and drew some tentative conclusions that corroborate the indices. First, the volume of such material in print did not really increase appreciably until the late 1950s. Advertisements were not effectively used until many years after the initial construction of special-purpose and early commercial machines. Second, these advertisements, like the articles, stressed that computers were interchangeable with calculators as a form of technology and that these machines were faster and more capable than earlier technologies. The authors of this study stressed that advertising writers used the analogy of the already familiar calculator to convey the concept of the computer to the general public to leave the message that these new devices were, as one IBM advertisement put it, "giant electronic calculators."[9] Not until the mid-1960s did such advertisements describe computers as information processors.[10] Like the articles, advertisements overstated the case, suggesting that technology was here and now; in short, computers in advertisements were more advanced than they really were at the time.[11] And as with many articles, the initial advertisements were aimed at potential users—scientists and very large businesses. Not until the late 1950s did manufacturers target commercial users in general through broad campaigns.

Informing the Buyer

Advertisements beg the question, How directly did the more detailed articles on computers affect potential buyers? What were they told? What was the message? Although some of these questions cannot be answered with certainty but deserve a book of their own, focusing on the publicly available message, nonetheless, contributes answers. The themes presented by publications are a useful vehicle for gauging the message. Publications almost uniformly conveyed a gospel of computing machines being "good," "smart," or "professional"; by the early 1960s they pitched computers as examples of "scientific principles" applied to management. Such advertisements were very reminiscent of similar messages evident in the years from 1910 to 1930 when accounting machine vendors spoke about "systems," "scientific management," and the application of technology.

During the early 1950s the business literature establishment discovered the computer, an event best exemplified by the *Harvard Business Review*'s publication of a series of articles on the use of electronics in business.[12] Potential users were exposed increasingly to articles on how others effectively used equipment within their particular industries. Trade journals began to publish material relevant to their narrower audiences to describe the use of this technology in familiar environments. That type of publication simply continued a genre that had existed since the late nineteenth century on the use of new technologies in offices, factories, and stores often in the same journals. The trade journals are of particular importance because their articles were more specific and serious than those that appeared in such magazines as *Time* or *Business Week*. Furthermore, the authors of the trade articles were either users of computers or potential buyers with whom other potential users could identify.

Most of the application-oriented articles of the 1940s focused on scientific uses of calculators and computers.[13] Operations research also received treatment as it migrated from war-related to more civilian uses.[14] Not until the 1950s, however, did articles begin to appear on the use of computers in accounting, the initial business application of the new technology.[15] In the 1950s many organizations and agencies— the American Association of Collegiate Registrars and Admissions Officers, the American Management Association, the U.S. Congress, General Electric, the American Bankers' Association, the Institute of Radio Engineers, the Controllership Foundation, and the Society of Actuaries[16]—looked at computers, reporting on their progress to their readers for reasons probably specific to their own needs. Other organizations and individuals published articles during the early 1950s on the use of computers in business, and by mid-decade the volume was rising, much as publications appeared for the general public. Articles appeared specifically on applications to business,[17] manufacturing,[18] government,[19] and society.[20] Books on computers also began to appear for the general public.[21]

Because of the potential for time-proven uses of accounting machines and punched-card equipment, it was almost to be expected that as soon as the public at large began reading about computers the use of these new machines would begin to receive considerable attention in publications aimed at possible users. The amount of literature that addressed possible uses and comparisons with previously available equipment grew by mid-decade. Emphasis lay typically on how to

Table 5.2

Sample of U.S. Trade Journals Printing Articles on Computers for the First Time, 1950–55

ACCOUNTING	PROCESS
Accounting Research	Gas
Accounting Review	Railway Age
Journal of Accountancy	World Petrolem
MANUFACTURING	PUBLIC SECTOR
Aero Digest	American City
Aviation Week	OTHER INDUSTRIES
Control Engineering	Business Week
Dun's Review	Fortune
Electrical Engineering	Nation
Electrical Manufacturing	Personnel Administration
Journal of Engineering Education	Research for Industry

displace clerical functions with these newer machines.[22] In the 1950s this type of publication appeared in profusion. Activity with computers had also increased, so much so that it drew the attention of the U.S. Department of Labor's Bureau of Labor Statistics, which joined the nearly century-old debate about whether or not office automation cost jobs; it concluded that it did not.[23] For those interested in knowing what applications made sense in the office, useful guides became available by mid-decade. One example from many was by R. Hunt Brown, published in 1955. Brown described available computers and recommended which ones should be installed for specific applications in accounting and science. His was a guide for managers who knew nothing about these first-generation computers.[24]

Samples of the hundreds of American trade journals carrying articles on computers for the first time in the 1950s are listed in Table 5.2. What becomes very obvious is the breadth of industries interested in the topic. Although more study of this type of literature is needed, it is important because many users of computers learned initially about these machines from such publications. The acquisition process began with a review of such literature, then went to more specialized publications, such as *Datamation,* vendor-held seminars, and, finally, to very detailed feasibility studies. *Datamation,* which began publication in 1957, played a major role in spreading information about computers in the 1960s.

Management books on data processing built on this early literature, citing cases of actual installations to describe how to select equipment, justify its cost, manage data centers, and install applications. Many of the recommendations on acquisitions, justification, use, and management reflected practices long evident in the office equipment market.[25] The advice given on justification generally suggested displacing clerical costs but gave almost no consideration to the creation of better information for management.[26] Although readers were told about the pros and cons of renting compared with purchase, little was done to measure the value of information. Justification of such expenses only began to appear during the late 1960s. It was assumed that organizations would continue to process the flow of information and to preserve their existing management structures as they had before the computer; little thought was given to what computers might do to either.[27]

Little is known about how the computer was introduced to the American public on the radio. Television images were few in the 1950s. Some commentary about computers began to appear in science fiction literature in the 1950s, but not in more traditional or widely read literature. That would begin to happen during the 1960s. Thus, the majority of material on the computer remained the purview of serious nonfiction and technical or business publications.

What impact did business and scientific literature and movies have on potential buyers in the early 1950s? Given the fact that there was almost no knowledge about computers at the start of the decade among potential buyers, writers on data processing had a large task before them. Donald Hart, who worked with General Motors on computer-related projects beginning in 1951, recalled that there were few even in that large firm who had any notion of the subject.[28] IBM's Cuthbert Hurd reported that one of the first things his company had to do to sell computers was to educate potential buyers.[29] IBM also published materials on the management of data-processing equipment to help the cause along[30] while its sales force had to learn about the new technology and then turn around and educate their customers through local seminars and national marketing programs.[31]

Two sources offer a glimmer of the effect: what managers of the period reported, and how many machines were actually installed. In both cases the conclusion reached by many in the early 1950s was that computers still had a ways to go. General Electric exemplifies the attitude of the period. Ironically, while GE was installing the first electronic digital computer dedicated totally to commercial applications (UNIVAC I in its Louisville, Kentucky, manufacturing plant) and receiving a great deal of publicity for this action in such a wide range of publications, from weekly news magazines to the prestigious *Harvard Business Review,*[32] it was circulating among its managers a detailed, sober report on computers and operations research that, although hopeful about the future of computers, did not reflect as positive an attitude toward them as existed in most publications.

On the question of how effective the literature was on the acceptance and use of computers, GE noted (ca. 1952):

> Unfortunately, most of this reporting falls in one of two classes, neither well suited for the individual interested in an appraisal of potentialities in his business:
>
> 1. The technical report which is so concerned with the details of a particular machine or process that it is unreadable except to the specialist.
> 2. The business or trade magazine report which either glamorizes the subject or uses the content as a springboard for apocryphal prophecy concerning the future nature of business operations.
>
> Very little is said concerning how these things may be accomplished.[33]

On the benefits in general of computers, the GE study reported:

> The great virtue of these engines is the inherent speed with which they operate and their resultant capability of handling great masses of data.
>
> The computer is so much faster at routine computational work that many problems otherwise insoluble in point of time are now feasible. The inherent speed also makes it possible to test a variety of assumptions where a direct answer is not possible without the waste of precious time in demonstrating by manual methods that the assumptions were either false or absurd.[34]

GE asked the question on the minds of many other potential users: When did a computer become more useful than punched-card equipment? The answer proposed by this GE report was: at the point when punched-card equipment could not handle the volume or the complexity of information.[35] Despite what proponents might argue, GE, which also became a computer vendor, cataloged a whole series of problems concerning the reliability of tube technology and the lack of trained personnel to use and manage computers, problems that had to be overcome before wide acceptance was possible.[36] Yet the report concluded that there were appropriate uses that GE's managers should consider: when direct labor in handling information could be reduced, when indirect labor could be eliminated, when "laborious and routine engineering and scientific problems" could be done faster or with fewer people, and when "what if" analysis could be performed for management.[37]

The effect of the growing volume of literature and, more importantly, internal experience at GE and other companies was reflected in business results. GE concluded that the majority of American companies are "not yet clamoring for this type of control. It must be sold on a piecemeal basis and on the basis of the vendor recognizing the opportunity rather than the customer sensing it."[38] To a large extent, that was frequently how computers were acquired in subsequent years.

The Buying Decision Process

Examining how computers were acquired in the 1950s delineates a critical process by which users learned about computers and installed them. What is also interesting is that almost every acquisition followed a similar path of decision making. During that process knowledge about these machines diffused extensively, particularly within the business communities of large corporations by the late 1950s. During the late 1940s, those having to learn enough about computers to acquire them included staffs and chiefs of civilian and military agencies within the U.S. government. Engineers and scientists, both within government and also outside in universities and in government-dependent corporations (e.g., the aerospace industry), looked at computers all during the late 1940s and early 1950s. Beginning in the early 1950s, however, major commercial enterprises also began to study the computer to determine its possible application. By the second half of the decade the largest number of potential customers looking at the computer was commercial. Because they ultimately diffused computers most widely in the economy, taking a brief look at how these customers acquired machines is instructive.

Regardless of whether someone was a government engineer or a corporate accounting manager, the overall process for acquiring a machine followed an essentially similar path. Someone would either read about these devices in the public press or in specialized trade journals, or be told about them, primarily by those building such machines.

These individuals ranged from senior management to accountants, but typically were mid-level staff. They would, then, visit the manufacturer to learn more, possibly attend a seminar, and, if all went well, come back to their enterprises, propose that a feasibility study be conducted, spend anywhere from three to four months to two years determining how such a machine might be used profitably, and gain approval to install one.

The heart of the effort was the systems study, an exercise that included cross-functional skills (e.g., technical and accounting), performed typically by staff who would be responsible for using the machine. Sometimes a vendor would also be represented. But computer suppliers were always intimately involved in the process by the early 1950s. They also had to invest considerable amounts of time and effort to close a sale. By the mid-1950s, with the widely available general-purpose computer, management shifted its attention away from asking vendors to build one-of-a-kind or specialized devices (e.g., as did the military with Whirlwind) and instead sought to use existing configurations of machines (as with the IBM 650).

Invariably, because of the enormous cost of these machines, the systems study fell to a committee appointed to do the analysis. These task forces were populated with engineers, who could understand (or learn to understand) the computer and its operations, and always included representatives from accounting to help cost-justify the equipment, which often ran into millions of dollars. Hosting executives ranged from plant managers to chief financial officers, although increasingly it was the executives who owned accounting or inventory management. The objectives of such a study, to use the words of a consultant of the mid-1950s, were "to determine a company's requirements for data processing, electronic or otherwise, and then to select that pattern of data processing which best fits the requirements."[39] The study would determine whether to replace an existing manual, or partly manual or automated, process or to find a new use. Some applications also called for significant reorganization of people and departments; thus, the consequences of those actions had to be taken into account.

Who performed these early studies? In addition to the constituencies described, committees were staffed usually with divisional and departmental employees, lower to middle management, and, rarely, with senior management, although these early decisions were always escalated to top management and even to boards of directors for final approvals.

Frequently, in these early days, consultants familiar with computers were brought in from outside the corporation. Some were borrowed from corporations with whom the interested party had contacts or were hired as true fee consultants. Some of the earliest computer consultants in the United States were John Diebold, Richard G. Canning, and growing numbers of experts in the well-established accounting and auditing firms. Many of these early experts went on to publish articles and books on how to acquire, use, and optimize computers.

Because of the costs and possible risks of failure, these studies were extensive and thorough. These committees produced studies that sometimes ran into hundreds of pages, took one year or longer to write, and included "preselling" various levels of management by educating them about the technology and its potential advantages. Often the actual application would be designed during this phase so that there would be an exact understanding of the capabilities of the machines. By the 1960s that extra step was increasingly abandoned, deemed unnecessary as confidence in "sizing" a machine grew.

In the early years, published information on computers came more frequently from trade publications than from technical journals in computing. Many articles on the use of computers first appeared in accounting journals and then industry-specific publications. The list in Table 5.2 of journals that published articles on computing in the 1950s exemplifies how broad the range of publications was. By the mid-1950s hundreds of articles had been published on the use of computers. Most of them also described the kind of process that their authors went through to acquire the equipment. After surveying hundreds of these articles, I have concluded that, like the popular press, the volume of publications targeted at commercial readers did not begin to increase substantially until the mid-1950s and then became the torrent that continues today. By mid-decade, in addition to the application briefs, one begins to see articles on how to acquire equipment.[40]

By the late 1950s one could begin to read articles that summarized numerous acquisition decisions. Until that time, most of the literature concerned one company's decisions. That trend continued, but articles on aggregation of decisions appeared by the end of the decade. For example, in the late 1950s a highly influential article appeared in the *Harvard Business Review*, entitled "Management in the 1980s," in which the authors argued that in the 1950s and continuing into the next generation, decisions to acquire were/would be based on management's desire to centralize decision making, expand control, and deal with a wider range of problems while simultaneously reducing the number of employees.[41]

Another important source of information were the various management associations that were either industry-specific (e.g., as in insurance and banking) or more general. Very active by the end of the decade was the American Management Association (AMA), which conducted seminars and published widely distributed articles and booklets on computing. For example, the AMA commissioned James D. Gallagher, a leading expert on business computing in the 1950s, to write a report on the subject. He advised readers how to make an acquisition, perform the feasibility study, and deal with vendors.[42] Others did the same thing.[43]

The news was not always positive. For instance, in 1958 John Diebold, already nationally recognized and highly visible for his writings and speeches in the business community on the general theme of automation, argued in *Dun's Review* that expectations for computing had not yet been realized.[44] Based on his survey of 280 users, he argued that the problem largely had been one of management underestimating the effort required to apply computers successfully. Yet, as did almost all other writers informing buyers about computers, he remained optimistic: "Though their initial enthusiasm may be dampened, few management men who have looked seriously into the potential of automation feel that anything short of a revolution is involved."[45]

The same discussion about how to acquire and use computers, and the actual results, received attention in British commercial publications.[46] In both countries, the publications most influential on management were probably trade journals, not data-processing publications or the national press, which was never specific enough on day-to-day management issues. The press simply caught managers' attention; data-processing publications (such as *Datamation*) either were not read outside of a small circle of computer experts in this early period or simply did not begin publication until late in the 1950s, by which time American business personnel were acquiring computers by the hundreds and then thousands.

To summarize the pattern of the 1940s and 1950s, in the earlier period—the 1940s to the early 1950s—technically proficient individuals (e.g., engineers and computer experts) working with middle management in scientific, engineering, and military communities, defined the case for acquiring computers based on intimate conversations with the actual builders of the machines (e.g., IBM, RCA, GE, ERA, Eckert and Mauchly). By the mid-1950s, interest in the commercial arena was strong, particularly for using such machines to automate further production, inventory control, and accounting, often building on previously successful uses of tabulating equipment. Feasibility studies were written, usually supervised by middle management but with the final decisions always made by senior executives. Information flowed to business through trade and industry publications and through running dialogues with vendors, such as those from IBM and, later, Burroughs, who taught seminars, hosted plant visits, and, by the end of the 1950s, had fielded sales forces capable of effectively selling such equipment. In the mid-1950s a body of literature appeared, published by these vendors, describing how computers could be used and featuring specific implementations by company or application and the rationale behind them. The archives of the major vendors today are filled with the remnants of these publications.[47] The older process, evident in the mid to late 1940s, of plant engineers talking to potential customer engineers had passed, replaced with a more recognizable marketing process.

Measurable Results

A long road lay between theoretical considerations and early implementation of computer technology, which began in the 1920s and 1930s, and actual construction of computers in the 1940s. The trail then extended from the end of World War II to the mid-1950s before computers realistically were commercially viable. Measurements on volumes document precisely the end of the journey from laboratory to user. A number of important questions related to results need to be asked about the process. How many computers were actually installed? What were they worth? How many people used them, let alone made them? In short, how much economic impact did they have on the office equipment industry and on the United States? Given the hype the birth of the computer has enjoyed in many accounts, from an economic point of view, when did they become measurably important? A number of calculations of equipment installations conducted by government officials, economists, and historians help answer these questions without requiring an extensive discussion. Their data also suggest that considerable progress had been made particularly from 1945 to 1955 in moving computers out of the laboratory and into the hands of users. The data provide strong evidence, however, that the "computer industry" or the "data-processing" (dependent on the use of computers) industry remained minuscule until the late 1950s.

In the United States immediately after World War II twenty non-profit organizations, primarily government and university laboratories, were involved in the construction of machines; a number of companies toyed with the new machines and, more frequently, with their component technology.[48] All the major surveys of computer populations begin with statistics from the mid-1950s, however, when there were enough machines to be significant. Flamm, for instance, was the latest to calculate the total worth of twelve companies playing the computer game in 1953–54; their sales were more than $3.6 billion. Yet that figure included all products from typewriters to calculators, adding machines to cash registers, and, thus, was information more useful in calculating the size of the office machines business as a whole.[49] Given that many had not even introduced their first computer product yet—for example, NCR, Minneapolis-Honeywell, RCA—the actual value of such devices had to be far less than this dollar amount. For 1950 Flamm counted 2 electronic digital computers in use in the United States and another 3 in Great Britain, bringing the worldwide total to 5. For 1955 his count reached 240 for the United States, 13 in Great Britain, and 5 each in France and Germany for a total of 263 systems worldwide.[50] Although his number for 1950 may be too low by as many as 2 to 4 machines, nonetheless, the growth in the total number of installations remained dramatic both in installation rate and absolute numbers.

The most detailed statistical counts on all aspects of the data-processing world for the 1950s through the 1970s came from Montgomery Phister, Jr., an industry consultant. He compiled massive, highly detailed tables of information that have been relied upon by investigators of the industry for more than a decade with relative confidence. Phister placed a value of $95 million on all computers, peripherals, software, telecommunications, and services for 1955. He believed these grew to $209 million in 1956 and to $324 million in 1957. In 1959 the revenues reached $719 million and nearly surpassed $1 billion in 1960.[51] His data included worldwide shipments by U.S. manufacturers. Phister suggested that in 1954 hardware shipments alone amounted to $10 million and grew to $600 million in 1959.[52] Each of his many tables showed minimal activity in the early 1950s when compared to the substantial growths in the late 1950s, especially beginning in 1956–57. For example, he identified ten computers owned by the U.S. government in 1954.[53] Software had a value too small to measure before the late 1950s and was of no statistical consequence until the 1960s. Furthermore, software was not separately priced in the earlier decade.[54] Service bureau work by the mid-1950s amounted to $15 million in value, but not all was done on computers; much continued to be done on tabulating gear, carrying on a tradition dating back to just after World War I.[55] When separating computers from total systems, he established that revenues for general-purpose computers from American manufacturers were $30 million in 1955, suggesting by implication that prior sales were vastly smaller. They grew from this figure to more than $5 billion annually in 1967 and $13 billion in 1974.[56] No reliable statistics are available for the period 1945–53, but historians know by name what machines were built in the United States, Great Britain, and France, and tentatively in Germany and less so for the Soviet Union. Commercial systems became available only in the early 1950s and, thus, were scarcely important when measured statistically either by industry dollar value or by absolute numbers installed until after 1953, and realistically not until after 1955.

The extensive debate that began in the 1970s among economists on the prices of computers need not detain the reader here. Largely, their concern has been over the phenomenon of how much the price of computing has declined unlike costs in many other industries, which actually rose.[57] All the controversy has been stirred up by various methods for measuring this trend across multiple technologies and generations of computers. To boil down the results to the actual outcome, however, over the forty years since the 1950s, the cost of computer horsepower has decreased between 22 percent and 26 percent each year, depending upon whose calculations you use. The most thorough of these studies, by Robert J. Gordon, suggests that for the period 1954–65, prices dropped by 22.1 percent, at nearly half that rate from 1965 to 1977, and, subsequently, by 26.5 percent with an overall average for all technologies over the entire period of approximately 20 percent.[58] The implication by economists is that the decline in cost of computers encouraged acquisition of these machines as opposed to another technology. That was definitely the case when customers replaced an earlier rental machine with another, but it is not clear whether the same applied in the 1950s. What did apply was whether a machine could do the work of older accounting devices or of people for less expense and with low risk of failure or breakdown.

As noted throughout this book, the acquisition of computers depended on a variety of factors of which price was only one component. Others included the price of peripheral equipment (some of which did not decline, such as printers and data entry equipment), salaries and overhead for personnel to operate equipment, programming expense, maintenance, availability of computer rooms, and the cost displacement of automating a process instead of using older methods. Yet the decline in prices is one of the most distinctive characteristics of the computer business. It was a phenomenon of no relevance in the period 1945–53 when all machines were experimental, one-of-a-kind, and built for government use. The early commercial devices were price sensitive but less so toward each other and more so in response either to production costs or to existing technological alternatives (e.g., adding and calculating equipment or punched-card tabulators).

By the end of the 1950s a sufficient number of commercial machines had been built to afford a track record of price declines. This trend was evident as new technologies drove down costs of computing. Because capacities also grew simultaneously, vendors were able to sell larger machines; therefore, a customer paid more for the next device than for the previous one even though the cost of, for example, performing a simple multiplication actually dropped by an average of 20 percent a year. The customer simply wanted to perform more transactions and, thus, required more "horsepower!"

Another way to examine the rate at which computers made their way into the general economy is to look at the number of people working with such machines. As noted earlier, several hundred people were involved at the end of World War II, and this group had grown to several thousand by the end of the decade.[59] Phister's data are not absolutely clear on the subject but, nonetheless, suggestive. Within the U.S. government, which was the largest user of office appliance technology, of the total 9.9 million personnel-years employed in 1955, some 6 million were dedicated to keypunching, an activity associated with both tabulating equipment and computers.[60] He estimated that more than six thousand keypunch operators were working for the government in 1955.[61]

Another source placed the total population of programmers in all segments of the U.S. economy—a real test of who used computers—at ten thousand in 1955 and at sixty thousand in 1960. These population figures have built into them the assumption that one thousand general-purpose computers were in use in the United States in 1955 and five thousand in 1960.[62] Although the population of computers seems inflated for 1955 and, hence, the population of programmers, the figures for 1960 appear consistent across various studies. The more salient point, however, is that data-processing professionals began to be identified as such by the mid-1950s, suggesting that computers were making their way into the economy at large by then, although in very small numbers.

Although the rise of the data-processing profession still awaits its historian, the subject is important because any measure of this profession's growth is an indicator of computer technology diffusion and the growth of computer literacy. The figures just cited obviously indicate when computer technology began to manifest itself in public. A quick look at associations within the industry is also useful because they fostered the transmission of information about the technology and offered support, education, and a means of creating an industry identity. Although the history of these associations lies outside the scope of this book, acknowledging their existence does not. The publication dates of the most obvious ones are cataloged in Table 5.3. Note that some existed before the computer and simply took responsibility for promoting information about the new technology, whereas others were direct outcomes of the new technology's existence.[63]

The value of discrete types of functions was also being established very early. Phister noted that in 1955 systems analysts in the United States made, on average, $154 per week, programmers $120, computer operators $88, and keypunch operators $62. Income maintained these relative levels for decades, with the systems analyst position always more expensive than any of the other three.[64] The operator functions evolved from tabulating days; the other two reflected the technical skills required to design and then program systems to run on computers.

On the manufacturing side of the personnel equation, Phister developed statistics that showed that in the United States by 1955, more than 3,700 individuals were involved in the manufacture, sale, and maintenance of computer equipment. That number jumped to 8,100 the following year and up to 12,000 in 1957. By the end of 1960, 23,600

Table 5.3

Founding Dates of Early Data-processing Organizations, 1937–60

Organization	Year
American Society for Information Science (ASIS)	1937
Association for Systems Management (ASM)	1944
Instrument Society of America (ISA)	1945
Association for Computing Machinery (ACM)	1947
Data Processing Management Association (DPMA)	1949
IEEE Computer Society (IEEE-CS)	1951
Society for Computer Simulation (SCS)	1952
SHARE	1955
UNIVAC Scientific Exchange (USE)	1955
GUIDE	1956
Joint Users Group (JUG)	Late 1950s
International Federation for Information Processing (IFIP)	1960

Note: Many of the best-known associations were formed in the 1960s. These include the American Federation of Information Processing Societies (1961), Association for Educational Data Systems (1962), CUBE (1962), DECUS (1961), Scientific Data Systems (1961), and Society for Information Display (1962). Others were created in the 1970s and 1980s as well.

were employed.[65] Comparable statistics do not exist for any European country for the same period. But given that the lion's share of all manufacturing and use was in the United States (more than 80 percent) the numbers for Europe had to have been very small until the 1960s. In Great Britain sales of computers by the three vendors—Ferranti, BTM, and ICT—were few through the mid-1950s and really did not gain appreciably until 1956. Not until 1960 did their combined volumes reach fifty systems.[66] Phister argued that 90 percent of the worldwide population of computers were of U.S. origin through the mid-1970s, which suggests that most of the personnel on the manufacturing side of the business must have been employed in the United States.[67]

How many computers were in use by nation per million population or by gross national product? The very limited available data strongly suggest that in the United States, by 1955, the number was minuscule. The estimated size of $10 million for the new sector in 1954–55 against a U.S. population of 162.4 million makes such a comparison irrelevant or, at least, premature when applied to the early or mid-1950s. In 1960 there were twenty-five processors per million Americans. That number jumped to one hundred per million Americans in about 1964. European statistics for the 1960s mirror those for the United States in the

1950s—almost irrelevant in size.[68] Another way to look at the data is to examine the number of computers in use per $1 billion of the U.S. gross national product. Not until mid-1958 did one reach five machines per $1 billion of GNP. To put that in perspective, in 1960 the number of machines per $1 billion had doubled; it doubled again by the end of 1962 and again in 1966 over that of 1962. For Europe, in comparison, the five machines per $1 billion measurement was reached in 1960, doubled in 1962, and again in 1965. That range of difference between the two continents remained the same throughout the 1960s.[69] That is, although Europe's absolute volumes were lower, its growth rate in computer acquisition closely tracked that of the United States.

But numbers alone do not suggest the full result of moving technology from laboratory to market. It was a new wave seen at the time as fundamental and as a vision of things to come, whether good or not. The uncertainty was captured well by the title of an article in *Collier's* in 1953: "Can a Mechanical Brain Replace You?"[70] The question was precipitated by the use of a UNIVAC I by CBS on election night, November 4, 1952, to predict the outcome of the presidential election. On the basis of early returns from twenty-seven states (3.4 million votes of an expected 60 million) at 8:30 P.M. EST the computer predicted the outcome to within four electoral votes.[71] Although historians have yet to assess fully or correctly the subsequent impact of the computer on American society, clearly, in the early 1950s people saw a change coming of considerable proportions.

On a narrower, more practical level, computers were gaining acceptance. In manufacturing, for instance, a computer's worth in design work was well understood by 1956.[72] One commentator of the period later noted that with the growing emphasis in the early 1950s on "operations research" and "management science" for better decision making, "the simultaneous development of computers has interacted quite fortuitously with these efforts."[73] He also confirmed that many of the users in Phister's statistics had been accustomed to mechanical data handling with punched-card technology.[74]

An indication that automation in general had yet to affect the American worker's job by the mid-1950s can be drawn from the fact that various labor leaders were not ill-disposed to the use of new technologies in general. The president of the CIO, Philip Murray, testified in 1955, "I do not know of a single solitary instance where a great technological gain has taken place in the United States that has actually thrown people out of work."[75] Walter Reuther, another highly influential labor leader, said he concurred, provided that technology was "properly handled."[76] By 1960, however, some labor leaders were becoming concerned, suggesting in the late 1950s that enough computers were making their way into the market to be worrisome. One small example indicates the fear behind Phister's numbers. Wallace Weber, president of Local 889 of the United Auto Workers Union, representing white collar office workers at Chrysler's plants, argued in 1960 that "three years ago Local 889 had 5,000 members. Now we have 4,000, and the loss mostly is due to the inroads of automation in offices." He predicted that "in the long run, this [increasing use of computers] may eliminate half our jobs."[77]

Summary

The American public was exposed to the new technology in phases. First, scientists and engineers working on computers shared information among themselves in the 1940s, and that community grew larger by the start of the 1950s. They first populated government agencies and universities then emerged in various laboratories of electronics and office appliance companies. Then began a period when the popular press began to describe the technology in the early 1950s. Often overstating the capabilities and benefits of such machines, they nonetheless made the public aware of them and in positive terms. This interpretation was very consistent with the generally favorable disposition of the American public toward technologies of all sorts.

From 1950 to 1955 the numbers of publications and machine installations were low; they grew sharply in the second half of the decade. In the 1960s a massive expansion of both publications and installations maintained this parallel expansion of awareness and use. It cannot be an accident, therefore, that awareness of the technology was tied to usage. Publications were introduced before significant adoptions of the computer. This sequence applied more to articles than to books, more to scholarly treatises than to advertisements, and, particularly, to trade journal activities.

Vendors and customers remained cautious for more than a decade before committing significantly to the new technology. And even here, the commitment was to extend traditional marketing and applications evident for decades with accounting equipment. In short, they simply replaced older machines used for accounting with computers used for more accounting. The major exceptions were in scientific, engineering, and military applications, which in many cases did represent new uses.

In the final analysis, the journey from laboratory to user had to include important consumer awareness if the technology were to begin to penetrate the economy deeply. Until that was accomplished, one could expect a device such as the computer to be merely interesting and not practical to a wide band of potential users.

6

Patterns in Office Equipment Technology

Examining computers as a form of technology and comparing their evolution as characteristic of "high-tech" evolutions of the twentieth century is not enlightening enough. This book started with the notion that migration of the computer from concept or need to commercially available product would be instructive about how technologies emerged. I have described obvious details so that those who understand other technologies could notice some comparisons and contrasts in their fields. For specialists in computer history it is important to appreciate the connection with earlier information-handling technologies. A lesson is there with the computer.

To elucidate common themes I compare patterns observed with the computer to those evident with other technologies that, in the eyes of those who used them, were closely parallel. Such a comparison helps answer a basic question: To what extent does a tool such as the computer build on the experience of using earlier machines for similar tasks? Someone figured out how to beat something with a rock and progressed to using a club, then a hammer, and, finally, a type of hammer; someone applied the same kind of logic to the computer.

Historians of technology agree that tools are not developed in the abstract, especially sophisticated implements. Indeed, if there is any consensus, it is that tools evolve in variety (novelty) and purpose one upon the other.[1] One must, for example, enjoy the benefits of black and white television before asking that the technology support color, as in the movies, or stereo sound. With business machines, the power of a word processor becomes more evident if the user is already familiar with the benefits and limitations of a typewriter.

In an earlier book I argued that long before the computer came, technologies were manipulating data and an industry existed to supply appropriate machines for this task.[2] The office appliance industry supplied such devices as typewriters, adding and calculating machines, cash registers, and punched-card equipment. The suppliers of such office equipment saw the computer ultimately as an extension of these earlier devices and adopted it, taking it away from laboratories, universities, specialized computer vendors, and electronics firms for their own and successfully bringing it to market. Because of that link with the past, comparing patterns of evolution and adoption between the computer and earlier office machines suggests patterns more universal than those evident with one machine (the computer) while acknowledging that more than technological considerations were at work (e.g., vendors and public perceptions). This "ethno-office" view discounts the effects of scientific and engineering sectors of the new business on purpose, even though they were still important, particularly in the very early 1950s.

Office Machines and Computers

Developers of machines ranging from the typewriter to the computer evolved increasingly from single individuals to teams of engineers, from work done literally on a kitchen table to projects carried out in world-class laboratories. The more complex or more expensive the equipment became, the less one saw a lone inventor at work. But always there were the exceptions: Thomas Edison with his laboratory in the nineteenth century, George Stibitz initially at the Bell Laboratories in the 1930s, and even the college students who developed microcomputers in the 1970s. But the pattern generally held; as office appliance technology became more complex, larger numbers of people had to be involved in its development.

Christopher Lathan Sholes (1819–90) in the 1860s worked on various models of what eventually became the first commercially viable typewriter of the 1870s. William Burroughs (1855–98) constructed an adding machine in the same period and spent the 1880s and 1890s refining his device. Although initial work on the punched-card tabulator was done by Herman Hollerith (1860–1929) in the 1880s, its complexity caused him to put together very quickly a small team to design

and construct whole systems. By World War I some equipment designers essentially enhanced existing base designs. At C-T-R (later IBM)
were James A. Bryce (1880–1949) and Frederick L. Fuller (1861–
1943). Fuller had designed cash registers for NCR, using existing patterns that he enhanced in the late 1800s and early 1900s, and
essentially did the same for tabulating equipment at C-T-R.[3] Bryce was
responsible for almost all of the innovations in punched-card equipment at IBM from the mid-1920s to the end of World War II.

By the 1920s, however, a shift occurred to more complex development work as major corporations began establishing research and development facilities stocked with hundreds of engineers and scientists
before World War II. Bell Labs opened its doors in 1925 as an amal-
gam of craft shops and development departments from around AT&T.
At about the same time, similar yet smaller facilities were set up at
plant locations at Burroughs, NCR, and IBM. In other industries the
same held true. GE, RCA, and DuPont, similar in that they all relied on
science and technology for new products, for example, did the same.
Universities also began to invest in engineering capabilities housed in
specialized laboratories linked to businesses looking for equipment and
R&D. For example, the Astronomical Laboratory at Columbia University was strongly supported by IBM with funds and equipment in
exchange for development work on tabulators and new scientific applications of such devices. MIT had established similar relations with the
military and utility companies. The University of Pennsylvania at Philadelphia, the city that in the early twentieth century was the radio
capital of the United States, had many engineers, some of whom
worked on computers for the army and with the cooperation and support of IBM, NCR, and GE. By the 1940s one also could see R&D
work for computers at RCA linked to the Institute for Advanced Studies while other projects were under way at Stanford and at Iowa State
College (later Iowa State University). Thus, the pattern of commercial
laboratories and teams developed on the one hand, while on the other,
closer bonds grew to university facilities and substantial government
funding.[4]

Inventors and developers best able to bring their products to market
were the earlier ones, probably because they had no choice. They had
to find manufacturing and capital and to develop methods of distribution. It quickly became obvious that they were better at developing
equipment than at marketing it, and they soon turned distribution over

to others more capable of selling their creations. This was true in every case early in the nineteenth century. By World War I the major lines of information-handling equipment—typewriters, cash registers, adding and calculating equipment, and punched-card devices—were housed in companies that could develop, refine, manufacture, distribute, and service these machines. By then, with minor exceptions, engineers developing machines specialized—first, by concentrating on refining existing technologies and, second, by focusing on specific subsets of machines. For example, at IBM's Endicott laboratory by the end of the 1920s were some engineers who were experts on printing mechanisms, others on tabulators, and still others on cards and papermaking. The one modern exception, and even then only for a short while, was the team of Eckert and Mauchly, who left the Moore School, started their own firm, built a number of machines, and, finally, sold their business to Remington Rand. They then completed work on the UNIVAC I for that enterprise. Enhancements to that machine and development of the UNIVAC II in the 1950s came about in the same context as for many other computers—with teams and corporate structures.

The manner in which invention, creation, or development of machines came about was remarkably uniform. In the initial development of machines, the first typewriter, cash register, or calculator, for example, the inventor had a good idea of what the machine should be used for and, therefore, designed it to satisfy that application. Once these machines were built, however, other applications emerged from the minds of developers or users, and, in turn, these new ideas served as design points for enhancements or other changes in the equipment. The result was that the form and configuration of both office and computer equipment evolved over time as users and vendors saw needs for changes. No radically new technologies ever emerged overnight. Applications served as the map to new functions. Thus, for instance, punched-card users insisted that computers also use cards, and even when computer builders added magnetic tape storage, they kept punched-card equipment as part of the system for more than thirty years.[5]

A second observable pattern was the inclination of engineers to use existing components to build on previous applications. Many examples exist from the typewriter to the computer. Sholes relied on the work of others dating back to the early 1700s. Both Burroughs, with his adding machine made in a humble machine shop in the 1880s, and Stibitz, with miscellaneous components at Bell Labs in the 1930s, built their initial devices in this fashion. The story of how early computers were constructed is often a tale of lashing existing parts together, particularly in the early phases. Familiar components available long before the computer included vacuum tubes, telephone relays, electricity, and cathode ray tubes. Even the transistor was available for nearly one decade before it was incorporated into computers; the same was true for integrated circuits. As late as the 1970s, early "inventors" of microcomputers built them entirely from existing electrical components. Their genius was in packaging these into a useful new device for which a prior need already existed.[6]

Once available components were applied (by the late 1940s) to the computer, the need for new technologies became urgent. This need encouraged development of magnetic storage media, the transistor as a practical component, and a variety of integrated circuits. Their development was driven specifically by the invention of high-performance electronic parts designed for use in computers.

Thus, the more complicated a device became, the more frequently one saw special modifications either to existing components or to manufacturing or next introduction of new parts and processes for manufacture. Factories that made typewriters and adding machines looked very different from those that manufactured computers. The latter often had craft rooms that developed uniquely shaped repair tools, screws, and bolts of unique sizes and shapes, while those kinds of components in adding machines of the 1800s, for example, used standard size screws and bolts. The computer of the 1990s still follows a century-old pattern. Standard size screws are in them; they use Honeywell thermostats like those installed in other industrial equipment and, increasingly, the same kind of fiber optics cabling used in telephone networks.

Cross-pollination of technologies was always a common feature in the progress from typewriter to computer. The keyboard first introduced on typewriters soon appeared on cash registers, adding machines, later tabulating equipment, and, finally, as part of consoles on computers. Some computers not made by IBM in the 1950s and 1960s even used IBM Selectric typewriters as their consoles! A typewriter and an adding machine had many of the same components, albeit shaped differently, and manufacturing was essentially the same. The lessons learned from creating, machining, and manufacturing sewing machines were applied to typewriters and adding machines.[7] By 1900 some companies made both types of office equipment in the same plant. Ideas developed by electrical firms, telephone companies, and office appliance vendors were constantly copied and borrowed all through the twentieth century. Firms applied components differently, and new uses, therefore, emerged. By the 1950s a pattern had also developed of formalizing the process through cross-licensing. Remington Rand and IBM cross-licensed their computer technologies in the 1950s, as had Powers and IBM in the 1930s and Remington Rand and some typewriter firms in the late 1800s.[8]

Cross-pollination also was early and consistently applied as a competitive strategy, sometimes in violation of patent law. Vendors used *retro-engineering,* or *reverse engineering;* that is, they acquired a competitor's product, took it apart to see how it was built, and then offered an almost duplicate product with either a few enhancements or at a lower price, thereby taking advantage of the other's R&D investment. This was a notorious practice with cash registers in the 1890s; as early as the 1880s Remington Rand faced the same problem from dozens of typewriter firms.[9] Although this was not a severe problem with the most sophisticated office equipment of the middle decades of the twentieth century, by the 1970s it appeared again with disk and tape drives and in the 1980s with microcomputer "clones."[10]

To what extent does complexity of machines build on experiences gained from older ones? Is there a direct line of evolution from typewriter to computer? Could the computer have developed if the adding machine had not been created first? These are important questions for historians of technology as well as for vendors interested in determining whether or not a market was ready for some new product. The issue is one of sophistication, much like the question, Can an individual appreciate the subtleties of a fine French meal without first learning a great deal about French food? The evidence presented in this book, and in my earlier study of the office appliance industry, suggests that one must know about French food before being able to appreciate fully the quality offered by a five-star French restaurant.[11]

But the experiences do not have to be direct or the same for every guest at the metaphorical French restaurant. They must, however, all share a common body of knowledge and sense of expectations. In the case of the office appliance it was necessary to have developed and used tabulating equipment for various applications to appreciate the potential commercial use of computers. Someone had to use computers with very small memories to recognize passionately the need for larger memories. Someone had to use tabulating equipment that did not print results on paper to require both IBM and Powers to develop printing tabulators that would conform to conventional accounting practices.[12] Someone had to use a typewriter designed to print words out of sight at the back of the machine to see the need for a typewriter that displayed what was typed on a sheet of paper in front of the user. Adding machines called for calculators, which, in turn, pointed to the need for huge increases in capacities, and, hence, to the electromechanical monsters built by Bush and Aiken.

At the level of what parts to put into a machine, the lineage is not as clear. It was common, for example, for engineers to reach outside their spheres of knowledge for components. For instance, radio parts were co-opted into computers in the 1930s and 1940s. Typewriters of the 1870s were designed and manufactured much like sewing machines, whereas punched-card concepts owed greatly to early-nineteenth-century looms. The key to use of components in new devices was the ability of the developer to remain aware of their existence in other business or science applications. That is why looking at scientific meetings, availability of technical journals, and the role of competition and wartime activities is so crucial to any understanding of how a technology moved from laboratory to market. Obviously, the easier it was to be aware of applicable components and their uses, the faster one could expect them to be applied in novel ways. That ability to build novel devices spurred demand for even more specialized components and, then, equipment.

In fact, that ability to specialize is a significant characteristic of all the information technologies available from the typewriter to the computer. Once a device had been in existence for one decade or more, variations multiplied, sometimes into dozens with hundreds of possible configurations. That was particularly true with adding, billing, accounting, tabulating, and cash register equipment from the late 1890s through the 1970s. By the 1960s the same pattern was discernible with computers. But even as early as 1950 computer builders spoke of machines intended for scientific or commercial use, of analog compared with digital design. By the end of the 1970s computing capability was being built and software written and embedded in other industrial and military devices (e.g., papermaking machinery, rockets, and space ships). At what point did a typewriter stop being a typewriter and become a billing machine? In old photographs it is obvious that they were close relatives. Or to call out a more contemporaneous example, at what point does a photocopy machine stop being a normal Xerox-like device and become either a printer or a telecommunications instrument (a FAX machine)? In short, the evidence is clear in each decade of office equipment design: they constantly built on each other. Regardless of the original parentage of the successful machine type, a propensity existed to borrow and merge continuously.

Business issues also appeared very similar from one period to another. Office machine vendors in the 1950s worried about how big the market was for computers, whereas computer start-up firms worried about being too small. For small firms the risk of building unprofitable products was enormous. To one degree or another that concern existed for all types of office equipment. All also experienced slow acceptance, which injected uncertainty into business plans. In each instance the new technology had to be introduced, its application explained along with benefits of use, and, then, training provided. When typewriters were first marketed, nobody knew how to type! Because people knew how to add, they accepted adding machines more easily, but firms such as Burroughs and Felt & Tarrant either had to develop training manuals or run hundreds of training schools. As computers came into use, the same issue came up again: Who knew what they were, how to use them, and why? In each instance from typewriters to computers, the degree of acceptance of a new product was tied to how well customers understood the benefits and use of the machines.

All successful marketing efforts had several common elements. First, vendors explained (sold) what the machines were and how they could be used. Second, a great deal of initial support was required until users had the skills needed to use the equipment. Third, formal training programs were frequently required. The one exception was the typewriter; by World War II training was best obtained from schools and colleges and no longer from vendors. Fourth, service organizations were necessarily close to the customer. That meant repair people had to be available in every state, store fronts in every major urban center, and, with the early computers, maintenance engineers in the same rooms as the machines.

Fifth, a public relations effort was crucial. NCR mailed millions of advertisements from the Dayton, Ohio, post office in the 1890s, approximately 25 percent of all third-class mail in that city. All widely distributed magazines in the United States have carried advertisements for office appliances from World War I to the present. Efforts had to be made to ensure that thousands of articles appeared in trade publications on the beneficial uses of typewriters, calculators, adding machines, tabulating equipment, cash registers, and computers in each decade of their existence.[13] In fact, the volume of publications rose sharply after a technology or device had reached the age of about ten years and remained extremely high for the next four decades. The computer seems to be an exception in that the volume of publications is actually still rising. On approximately the fifteenth anniversary of the microcomputer, for example, more than 150 magazines devoted to this device existed worldwide.[14]

Office machines became very profitable when sold in volume. In each instance, vendors sought to standardize manufacturing and distribution and for each class of device were very successful. Although individual companies either were more successful or failed, as a whole these device types returned consistent profits one decade after another once significant volumes were achieved: the smaller and less complicated the device, the more copies that had to be sold, and the more sophisticated a machine, the more the opposite held true. This meant, for example, that by 1900 the business of a typewriter vendor could be very profitable, selling tens of thousands of machines yearly. The same applied to adding and calculating equipment. For tabulating machines thousands or even just hundreds satisfied the need for profitability. In the 1950s it was difficult to make a profit on dozens of computers but easy on hundreds. As competition within a particular device's market intensified, the volume required to make a profit rose because, in part, a vendor's response to competitors was through price reductions, which required greater manufacturing efficiencies. This clearly was the case with each device type and has continued to the present with microcomputers. Hand-held calculators illustrated the extent to which this could happen. In the early 1970s Hewlett-Packard sold a device for $700. The same function became available on Texas Instruments' products by 1976 for approximately $90, and, by the end of the 1980s, programmable calculators sold for $50. Simpler devices that just performed the four basic mathematical functions, calculated interests, and had memory could be purchased in the 1990s for as little as $3 and had shrunk from a large handful to a device the size of a credit card.

The Computer and the Office Appliance Industry

The connections between the computer and old office appliance technologies and the computer's position as the latest technology incorporated into the industry offer an opportunity to explore the general question of what effect a new technology has on an existing industry.

As with any new set of products, the computer business started small in ways that changed later. In 1950 few companies other than the Electronic Computer Company (Elecom) and Computer Research Corporation (CRC) were attempting to sell computers commercially; by 1955 some fifteen U.S. and one British firm had installed computers for nonmilitary purposes. These early enterprises were often tied to U.S. defense work, frequently located in the same community as a major university, and had strong skills in electronics and no ties to the office equipment world. But between the late 1940s and the mid-1950s the office equipment industry came to dominate the manufacture and sale of existing commercial computers (chapter 4). Office equipment vendors, not small computer firms staffed with engineers and few or no marketing personnel, created commercial markets for computers.

The process of taking over the market was relatively straightforward. Firms like IBM and Remington Rand acquired technical skills as part of doing business with the U.S. military during both World War II and the Korean War. The U.S. government asked them, in turn, to take on computer-related projects, which it funded. Finally, armed with potential products, a sales force, manufacturing capability, and a customer base most suited to use computers, it was easy to add such machines to the product line when the timing was right. In turn, that process heated up demand, which reinforced initial forays into the market and led dominant companies such as IBM and Sperry to invest more and introduce additional computer products. Their knowledge of the office world and ability to bridge old technologies with newer ones was a workable symbiotic relationship that resulted in the acceptance of computers by long-standing customers of the industry.[15] In short, the largest office equipment vendors had the capital and knowledge of the information-handling business to sell computers profitably.

But at the time electronics, small computer manufacturers, and aviation companies were the first enterprises to display a strong interest in commercial computers. Their attraction grew out of experiences like those of office equipment vendors; they, too, had developed expertise and worked for the U.S. military. But they lacked the customer base to sell to or the kind of appreciation needed to translate computer technology into practical commercial products for wide use in offices and factories. The real market consisted of hundreds of thousands of commercial enterprises employing millions of workers, not just the military or a few universities. Only the office equipment vendors were able to do the job. Yet in the early days of the computer large electronic firms appeared better positioned to compete (e.g., GE, Sylvania, and RCA). Well-run office equipment vendors moved effectively and, by the late 1950s, quickly dominated the fledgling business worldwide. Electronics firms came in and out of the business over the next four decades but with little success. European and Asian firms were also late entering the market, in effect leaving it to such companies as IBM, Sperry, and Burroughs to dominate throughout the 1960s and into the 1970s.

Another feature of the computer's effect was the compulsion evident on the part of many American office equipment vendors to enter the market by the mid-1950s. As sales of UNIVACs and IBM 701s and 650s accelerated in the mid-1950s, it became obvious to other vendors that if they, too, did not sell computers, their installed base of large accounting machines would be displaced by the likes of IBM and Sperry. As a self-protective and reactive act, therefore, they saw the need to participate in the new market by the late 1950s; many had entered by the early 1950s. That many of them did so ineffectively is another issue, but their recognition of the need to participate simply strengthened the process by which computers were fully integrated into the office equipment industry.

Ironically, history seemed to repeat itself. IBM, for instance, had been able to seize a large share of the punched-card market in the 1920s because of good marketing, corporate structure stabilized earlier than that of its rivals, and, by the end of the 1930s, sufficient capital and critical mass to support the product line against all competitors. In the 1950s it again was armed with capital, reasonably good marketing and sales resources, and technical expertise, and effectively challenged rivals sooner rather than later. Although companies such as Underwood, Monroe, Olivetti, and Bull introduced computers in the 1950s, they were either weak financially or less effective in marketing them than was IBM.

Larger firms also quickly acquired the expertise they needed. Remington Rand, Burroughs, NCR, and others bought talent to move rapidly into the business. Those not able to do so found the new market too expensive to enter. Underwood, for example, risked financial disaster as it attempted to develop its own computer product line. Small rivals, in time, were also neutralized by mergers when not defeated outright by failure. So the market landscape became less cluttered. Monroe and Marchant, respectively, folded into Litton and Smith-Corona; Underwood's computer business went to Olivetti; Remington Rand became part of Sperry. The same happened with electronic firms. Of the eleven companies working on commercial computers in the United States before 1955, four were acquired by office equipment vendors by 1955, five simply stopped developing computer products, while two lingered (J. B. Rea and Teleregister) for years before disappearing.[16]

One important observation made repeatedly in this book is that the computer business remained a relatively minor one until the late 1950s and even then proved less significant than has been implied by other writers. From the perspective of hindsight it seems logical that in time the office equipment industry assumed control over the development and marketing of computer equipment. That result appears reasonable because, as with all technologies, in the final analysis it is the use to which something is put that determines its destiny. Computers, initially, were the next round of technologies introduced to handle information and were perceived as such by users. That perception placed computers historically in a continuum of machines under development since the mid nineteenth century aimed specifically at improving the efficiency and speed with which information was gathered and used by both scientific/engineering and commercial users. Viewed that way, who initially developed the computer is less important than who ultimately came to sell or buy it.

The computer came into an industry with long-established roots in the American economy. Before the computer, data processing in America had an important history and its practices became those of the early computer market, giving it many of the characteristics evident in the late twentieth century. The computer's journey from laboratory to market also mirrored the path taken by many complex technologies in the twentieth century.

Some Concluding Thoughts on Patterns

Throughout this book I have presented an account of how computer technology was first developed and manufactured, how the American public first heard about it, and how both engineers/computer scientists and customers learned about the technology. I defined the role of various types of vendors—particularly those of the old office equipment industry—as the commercial vehicle required to transport this new technology to the far corners of the world's economy.

The story presented, as phases ranging first from activities in laboratories to awareness and finally to commercial success, may seem more a collection of anecdotes than part of a well-connected paradigm. In reality, however, events often occurred in complete isolation from others; the opposite was equally true. Cause-and-effect relationships were not necessarily obvious at the time. They are more neatly the product of industry observers after the fact. Historians, including readers of this book in manuscript form, and especially economists, have constantly sought to create elegant theses or models to explain what happened. Links, however, were always messy at best and never clear. What was obvious at the time, however, and clearer today, is that nobody had a master plan, a road map. All felt their way along as best they could, usually building on the activities of others who had come before them.

I began this book by arguing that the story of the computer contributes to a better understanding of the evolution of complex technologies in the twentieth century. Others studying aerospace or nuclear developments, for example, will have to judge for themselves the validity of this perspective. Some obvious points of similarity exist:

1. The base technologies built on nineteenth-century scientific studies.
2. As science was moved to technological applications, many people working in teams at universities and within companies were required in order to produce useful devices.
3. Scarcely any significant technology of the twentieth century came into existence without an extraordinary investment in it by national

governments. This was particularly pronounced in the United States in the period 1930–60. After 1960, the dynamics began to change as, for example, the Japanese and, to a lesser extent, the Europeans, invested in strategic technologies and their associated industries—a subject outside the scope of this book.

4. The transfer of technology to widespread use required adoption of this technology by preexisting corporations, although start-up enterprises provided initial commercial leadership.

5. Public awareness of a particular technology occurred at approximately the same time that the technology moved from being highly specialized (e.g., only for military or scientific uses) to commercially applicable. Related to this is the strong role played by print media in getting the word out to both the public at large and to buyers through widely distributed publications and narrowly focused trade and industry journals touting the wonders of the new technologies.

The computer had particular characteristics that distinguished it from other technologies. For one thing, it ultimately joined the mainstream of office applications, hence, my conscious effort throughout this book to link office appliances to computers to a far greater extent than have previous historians. The link was no accident. In addition, this technology became widely applied to other technologies that one would be tempted to use for comparison, such as airplanes and military equipment. People simply did not use as many rockets and spaceships on a daily basis as they did computers. No perfect paradigm exists, however, to describe technology transfer: each device has some unique characteristics over and above general observations. This would be as true for computers as it is for the telephone, television, automobile, airplane, and a host of other devices. Less understood are questions about the influence of various technologies. Some generalities on the issue of computer impact on society as a general indicator of possible patterns of behavior of any twentieth-century technology would be welcome because they could enhance appreciation for how technologies go from laboratory to market. But historians are too close to many of these technologies, and it is, perhaps, still too early in their life cycles to see patterns correctly. They have enough to do just tracking the emergence of specific technologies. But social historians want answers; they will have to provide them in time.

Economists have come closer to identifying common patterns of technology behavior than historians of either technology or society. They recognize the profound need for capital, for example, to make it possible for a technology to move out of the laboratory to market.[17] They have also begun to identify national patterns of investment in technologies as a critical cause of specific devices coming to the fore in one nation rather than another. The work done, for example, in comparing and contrasting Japanese, U.S., and European investments in technological development crosses many devices, and is not limited to computers.[18] Patterns exist, suggesting that government investment strategies have a direct correlation to technological developments, especially in military-related spheres.

I focused in this book more closely on the interrelationships among technology's developers, supporters, vendors, and the public/customers at large to provide a different and more specific view of a technology because economists have a tendency to oversimplify cause and effect and to find economic imperatives as the overwhelming influence on a course of events. Yet technology goes from laboratory to market along a complicated, long, and crowded path.

Notes

Preface

1. George Basalla, *The Evolution of Technology* (Cambridge: Cambridge University Press, 1988).

2. John M. Staudenmaier, "Comment: Recent Trends in the History of Technology," *American Historical Review* 95, no. 2 (June 1990): 715–25.

3. John B. Rae, *The American Automobile* (Chicago: University of Chicago Press, 1965); D. S. L. Cardwell, *Turning Points in Western Technology* (Canton, Mass.: Science History Publications, 1991); on telephony, for example, see A. E. Joel, Jr., et al., *A History of Engineering and Science in the Bell System: Switching Technology (1925–1975)* (n.p.: Bell Telephone Laboratories, Inc., 1982), one of six volumes on this laboratory and its technology; Joseph H. Udelson, *The Great Television Race: A History of the American Television Industry, 1925–1941* (University: University of Alabama Press, 1982).

4. Paul E. Ceruzzi, *Reckoners: The Prehistory of the Digital Computer, from Relays to the Stored Program Concept, 1935–1945* (Westport, Conn.: Greenwood Press, 1983).

5. James W. Cortada, *Before the Computer: IBM, NCR, Burroughs, and Remington Rand and the Industry They Created, 1865–1956* (Princeton, N.J.: Princeton University Press, 1993).

Chapter 1

1. John M. Staudenmaier, "Comment: Recent Trends in the History of Technology," *American Historical Review* 95, no. 2 (June 1990): 715–25.

2. Ibid.; Thomas S. Kuhn, *The Structure of Scientific Revolutions,* 2d ed. (New York: New American Library, 1986); I. Bernard Cohen, *Revolution in Science* (Cambridge, Mass.: Harvard University Press, 1985).

3. David S. Landes, *Revolution in Time: Clocks and the Making of the Modern World* (Cambridge, Mass.: Harvard University Press, 1983).

4. Elizabeth L. Eisenstein, *The Printing Press as an Agent of Change: Communications and Cultural Transformations in Early Modern Europe,* 2 vols.

(Cambridge: Cambridge University Press, 1979); Lucien Febvre and Henri-Jean Martin, *The Coming of the Book: The Impact of Printing, 1450–1800* (London: NLB, 1976); Warren Chappell, *A Short History of the Printed Word* (New York: Dorset Press, 1970).

5. For useful introductions to the literature see Charles Singer, E. J. Holmyard, and A. R. Hall, *A History of Technology*, 5 vols. (London: Oxford University Press, 1954–58); D. S. L. Cardwell, *Turning Points in Western Technology* (Canton, Mass.: Science History Publications, 1972); Merritt Roe Smith, ed., *Military Enterprise and Technological Change: Perspectives on the American Experience* (Cambridge, Mass.: MIT Press, 1985).

6. For a detailed bibliography of these kinds of histories see James W. Cortada, *A Bibliographic Guide to the History of Computing, Computers, and the Information Processing Industry* (Westport, Conn.: Greenwood Press, 1990), 188–342.

7. Daniel R. Headrick, *The Tools of Empire: Technology and European Imperialism in the Nineteenth Century* (New York: Oxford University Press, 1981); idem, *The Tentacles of Progress: Technology Transfer in the Age of Imperialism, 1850–1940* (New York: Oxford University Press, 1988); idem, *The Invisible Weapon: Telecommunications and International Politics, 1851–1945* (New York: Oxford University Press, 1991).

8. Kenneth Flamm has studied the example of the computer and government support in *Targeting the Computer: Government Support and International Competition* (Washington, D.C.: Brookings Institution, 1987); and idem, *Creating the Computer: Government, Industry, and High Technology* (Washington, D.C.: Brookings Institution, 1988).

9. Edwin Layton, "Mirror-Image Twins: The Communities of Science and Technology in 19th Century America," *Technology and Culture* 12, no. 4 (October 1971): 565; and idem, "Technology as Knowledge," ibid. 15, no. 1 (January 1974): 31–41.

10. Eda Kranakis, "Science and Technology as Intersecting Socio-Cognitive Worlds," in *Conference on Critical Problems and Research Frontiers in History of Science and History of Technology,* October 30–November 3, 1991 (Madison, Wis.: n.p., 1991), 1 [these proceedings hereafter cited as MADISON].

11. Robert Marc Friedman, *Appropriating the Weather: Vilhelm Bierknes and the Construction of a Modern Meteorology* (Ithaca, N.Y.: Cornell University Press, 1989); Crosbie Smith and M. Norton Wise, *Energy and Empire: A Biographical Study of Lord Kelvin* (Cambridge: Cambridge University Press, 1989); George Wise, Willis R. Whitney, *General Electric, and the Origins of U.S. Industrial Research* (New York: Columbia University Press, 1985); Kranakis, "Science and Technology," MADISON, 6.

12. Carl Mitcham, "Histories of Technology and Their Philosophies," MADISON, 9–24; Robert P. Multhauf, "Some Observations on the State of the History of Technology," *Technology and Culture* 15, no. 1 (January 1974): 1–12; Reinhard Rurup, "Historians and Modern Technology: Reflections on the Development and Current Problems of the History of Technology," ibid., 15, no. 2 (April 1974): 161–93; Melvin Kranzberg and Carroll Pursell, Jr., eds., *Technology in Western Civilization* (New York: Oxford University Press, 1967); Staudenmaier, "Comment: Recent Trends," 715–25.

13. Philip Scranton, "Determinism and Indeterminacy in the History of Technology," MADISON, 25–41, also has an excellent bibliography on the subject, which has drawn the attention of many historians.

14. Cortada, *Before the Computer,* see part 1 on pre-1920 events.

15. Daniel R. Headrick, "The Sources of Technological Innovation in the Armed Forces: The Case of the U.S. Navy, 1865–1915," MADISON, 282–89.

16. David F. Noble, *Forces of Production: A Social History of Industrial Automation* (New York: Oxford University Press, 1986).

17. Headrick, "Sources," 287.

18. James R. Beniger, *The Control Revolution: Technological and Economic Origins of the Information Society* (Cambridge, Mass.: Harvard University Press, 1986).

19. David A. Hounshell and John Kenly Smith, Jr., *Science and Corporate Strategy: DuPont R&D, 1902–1980* (Cambridge: Cambridge University Press, 1988), 1–2, 593–601.

20. Robert Sobel, *IBM: Colossus in Transition* (New York: Times Books, 1981), 70–95. Charles J. Bashe, Lyle R. Johnson, and John H. Palmer, *IBM's Early Computers* (Cambridge, Mass.: MIT Press, 1986); and Emerson W. Pugh, Lyle R. Johnson, and John H. Palmer, *IBM's 360 and Early 370 Systems* (Cambridge, Mass.: MIT Press, 1991), are excellent histories of corporate technology.

21. Alfred D. Chandler, Jr., *The Visible Hand: The Managerial Revolution in American Business* (Cambridge, Mass.: Harvard University Press, 1977); but also see idem, *Scale and Scope: The Dynamics of Industrial Capitalism* (Cambridge, Mass.: Harvard University Press, 1990).

22. David S. Landes, *The Unbound Prometheus: Technological Change and Industrial Development in Western Europe from 1750 to the Present* (Cambridge: Cambridge University Press, 1969), 538. I argue that such ordering up, although it exists, is not as easily achieved as he implies or as one sees in this case study of how early computers were built.

23. Ibid., 538–55.

24. Cardwell, *Turning Points in Western Technology,* 218.

25. George Basalla, *The Evolution of Technology* (Cambridge: Cambridge University Press, 1988), vii.

26. Ibid., 45.

27. Ibid.

28. Ibid., 91; Cortada, *Before the Computer;* see, especially, part 2 on the period between the two world wars.

29. Basalla, *Evolution of Technology,* 91.

30. Jacob Schmookler, *Invention and Economic Growth* (Cambridge, Mass.: Harvard University Press, 1966).

31. Flamm, *Creating the Computer,* 29–79; Barton C. Hacker surveys the literature in "On the History of Military Technology," MADISON, 290–309.

Chapter 2

1. I. Bernard Cohen, *Revolution in Science* (Cambridge, Mass.: Harvard University Press, 1985), 96.

2. The bibliography is summarized in James W. Cortada, *A Bibliographic Guide to the History of Computing, Computers, and the Information Processing Industry* (Westport, Conn.: Greenwood Press, 1990), 66–187; Michael R. Williams, *A History of Computing Technology* (Englewood Cliffs, N.J.: Prentice-Hall, 1985), 213–381.

3. Williams, *A History of Computing Technology,* 213–381; David Ritche, *The Computer Pioneers: The Making of the Modern Computer* (New York: Simon and Schuster, 1986); Joel Shurkin, *Engines of the Mind: A History of the Computer* (New York: W. W. Norton, 1986); G. Harry Stine, *The Untold Story of the Computer Revolution: Bits, Bytes, Bauds, and Brains* (New York: Arbor House, 1985), are recent examples.

4. Kenneth Flamm, *Creating the Computer: Government, Industry, and High Technology* (Washington, D.C.: Brookings Institution, 1988); Franklin M. Fisher, James W. McKie, and Richard B. Mancke, *IBM and the U.S. Data Processing Industry: An Economic History* (New York: Praeger, 1983); James R. Beniger, *The Control Revolution: Technological and Economic Origins of the Information Society* (Cambridge, Mass.: Harvard University Press, 1986), are examples.

5. For instance, most of the authors contributing to L. Wexelblat, ed., *History of Programming Languages* (New York: Academic Press, 1981); and to N. Metropolis, J. Howlett, and Gian-Carlo Rota, eds., *A History of Computing in the Twentieth Century* (New York: Academic Press, 1980), are scientists or engineers who were present at the creation. Other titles and authors include Emerson W. Pugh, *Memories that Shaped an Industry: Decisions Leading to IBM System/360* (Cambridge, Mass.: MIT Press, 1984) (engineer); Nancy Stern, *From ENIAC to UNIVAC: An Appraisal of the Eckert-Mauchly Computers* (Bedford, Mass.: Digital Press, 1981) (professor of computer science); among writers and journalists see David Ritchie, *The Computer Pioneers* (New York: Simon and Schuster, 1986); Katharine Davis Fishman, *The Computer Establishment* (New York: Harper & Row, 1981); Pamela McCorduck, *The Universal Machine: Confessions of a Technological Optimist* (New York: McGraw-Hill, 1985); among economists see Fisher, McKie, and Mancke, *IBM and the U.S. Data Processing Industry;* William F. Sharpe, *The Economics of Computers* (New York: Columbia University Press, 1969); Richard Thomas DeLamarter, *Big Blue: IBM's Use and Abuse of Power* (New York: Dodd, Mead, 1986); and among historians see Paul E. Ceruzzi, *Reckoners: The Prehistory of the Digital Computer, from Relays to the Stored Program Concept, 1935–1945* (Westport, Conn.: Greenwood Press, 1983); Robert Sobel, *IBM: Colossus in Transition* (New York: Times Books, 1981); and James W. Cortada, *Historical Dictionary of Data Processing,* 3 vols. (Westport, Conn.: Greenwood Press, 1987). The smallest bibliography is that of professionally trained historians.

6. Charles J. Bashe, Lyle R. Johnson, and John H. Palmer, *IBM's Early Computers* (Cambridge, Mass.: MIT Press, 1986), 145–46, 159–61, 265–67, 406–11; William E. Harding, "Semiconductor Manufacturing in IBM, 1957 to the Present: A Perspective," *IBM Journal of Research and Development* 25, no. 5 (September 1981): 647–58.

7. Flamm, *Creating the Computer,* comes closest to putting the story of institutional support in broad perspective.

8. For examples of this analysis see W. S. Bagby, "Deciding upon an Elec-

tronic Data-Processing System," *The Controller* 24 (May 1956): 216–21; J. D. Elliott, "EDP—Its Impact on Jobs, Procedures and People," *Journal of Industrial Engineering* 9, no. 5 (September–October 1958): 407–10; Ida Russalkoff Hoos, "When the Computer Takes Over the Office," *Harvard Business Review* 38, no. 4 (July–August 1960): 102–12.

9. Montgomery Phister, Jr., *Data Processing Technology and Economics* (Santa Monica, Ca.: Santa Monica Publishing, 1976), 332.

10. Kenneth Flamm, *Targeting the Computer: Government Support and International Competition* (Washington, D.C.: Brookings Institution, 1987), 125–72.

11. Ibid. On the Japanese situation, see Marie Anchordoguy, *Computers Inc.: Japan's Challenge to IBM* (Cambridge, Mass.: Council on East Asian Studies, Harvard University, 1989).

12. For a sampling, see Beniger, *Control Revolution;* Dirk Hanson, *The New Alchemists: Silicon Valley and the Microelectronics Revolution* (Boston: Little, Brown, 1982); Ernest Braun and Stuart Macdonald, *Revolution in Miniature: The History and Impact of Semiconductor Electronics* (Cambridge: Cambridge University Press, 1982); Jacques Vallee, *The Network Revolution* (Berkeley: AND/OR Press, 1982); Tom Logsdon, *The Robot Revolution* (New York: Simon and Schuster, 1984); Stine, *Untold Story of the Computer Revolution.*

13. Cohen, *Revolution in Science,* 10.

14. The notion is explained in Hanson, *New Alchemists,* 1–38.

15. A useful early expression of the notion as applied to early technological innovations can be found in H. S. Harrison, "Discovery, Invention, and Diffusion," in Charles Singer, E. J. Holmyard, and A. R. Hall, eds., *A History of Technology,* 5 vols. (Oxford: Oxford University Press, 1954), 1:66–77; Hanson, *New Alchemists,* 3–69; for the example of data processing see Flamm, *Creating the Computer,* 3, 12–23.

16. Cohen, *Revolution in Science,* 20.

17. Braun and Macdonald, *Revolution in Miniature,* 9–44.

18. Cohen, *Revolution in Science,* 20–21. This characteristic was also illustrated by T. P. Hughes, *Networks of Power: Electrification in Western Society, 1880–1930* (Baltimore: Johns Hopkins University Press, 1983).

19. David F. Noble, *America by Design: Science, Technology and the Rise of Corporate Capitalism* (New York: Alfred A. Knopf, 1977), describes the process.

20. Hanson, *New Alchemists,* 3–38.

21. W. W. Dalton, *This Story of Radio,* 3 vols. (London: British Book Centre, 1976).

22. Maurice Wilkes, famed British computer builder, noted in his memoirs that radio "laid the foundation of my knowledge of electronics," *Memoirs of a Computer Pioneer* (Cambridge, Mass.: MIT Press, 1985), 5; Herman Lukoff, who participated in the building of the UNIVAC, noted in his memoirs the influence of radio and dedicated a whole chapter to the subject in *From Dits to Bits: A Personal History of the Electronic Computer* (Portland, Ore.: Robotics Press, 1979), 8–15; An Wang, an early developer of computer memory, also described his early work with and debt to radio in his memoirs, *Lessons: An Autobiography* (Reading, Mass.: Addison-Wesley, 1986), 27–28. Herman H. Goldstine, *The Computer from Pascal to Von Neumann* (Princeton, N.J.: Princeton University Press, 1972), 237–39.

23. Bashe, Johnson, and Palmer, *IBM's Early Computers,* 34–72.

24. Carl B. Boyer, *A History of Mathematics* (Princeton, N.J.: Princeton University Press, 1968), 55–76; I. M. Bochenski, *A History of Formal Logic,* trans. Ivo Thomas (Notre Dame, Ind.: University of Notre Dame Press, 1961).

25. Goldstine, *Computer from Pascal to Von Neumann,* 35–38.

26. For example, W. H. Eccles and F. W. Jordan, "A Trigger Relay Utilising Three-Electrode Thermionic Vacuum Tubes," *Radio Review* 1 (1919): 143–46; H. H. Suplee, "The Principle of Reversal: A Suggestion for Inventors," *Scientific American* 109 (November 1, 1913): 344.

27. McCorduck, *Machines Who Think,* 46, 68; C. E. Shannon, "Mathematical Theory of Communications," *Bell System Technical Journal* 27 (July 1948): 379, 623; and a much later piece that he wrote with E. F. Moore, "Reliable Circuits Using Less Reliable Relays," *Journal of Franklin Institute* 262 (September 1956): 191.

28. A relay is an electromagnet with a stationary electrical contact that is movable with a spring. The contact operates like a telegraph key. Relays either open or close the electrical circuit. These relays were used in various combinations in direct-dialing telephone systems during the early decades of the twentieth century.

29. Claude E. Shannon's master's thesis was published as "A Symbolic Analysis of Relay and Switching Circuits," in Earl E. Swartzlander, Jr., ed., *Computer Design Development: Principal Papers,* (Rochelle Park, N.J.: Hayden, 1976), 3–24, and originally appeared in *Transactions of the AIEEE* 57 (1938): 712–13.

30. A. M. Turing's famous paper was published as "On Computable Numbers, with an Application to the Entscheidungs-problem," *Proceedings of the London Mathematical Society,* ser., no. 2, 42 (1937): 230; for an analysis of his work see Andrew Hodges, *Alan Turing: The Enigma* (New York: Simon and Schuster, 1983): 96–99, 105–10.

31. Allen W. M. Coombs, "The Making of Colossus," *Annals of the History of Computing* 5, no. 3 (July 1983): 253–59; Hodges, *Alan Turing,* 267–68, 277–78, 292–94.

32. Goldstine, *Computer from Pascal to Von Neumann;* William Aspray and Arthur Burks, eds., *Papers of John Von Neumann on Computing and Computer Theory* (Cambridge, Mass.: MIT Press, 1987), xiv.

33. The paper is conveniently reprinted in Aspray and Burks, *Papers of John Von Neumann,* 17–82; and for an analysis of the paper see Donald E. Knuth, "Von Neumann's First Computer Program," *Computing Surveys* 2, no. 4 (December 1970): 247–60; also reprinted in Aspray and Burks, *Papers of John Von Neumann,* 83–96.

34. On his views and influence, William Aspray, "The Mathematical Reception of the Modern Computer: John Von Neumann and the Institute for Advanced Study Computer," in Esther R. Phillips, ed., *Studies in the History of Mathematics,* vol. 26 of *Studies in Mathematics* (Washington, D.C.: Mathematical Association of America, 1987), 166–94; but also see Aspray's biography, *John Von Neumann and the Origins of Modern Computing* (Cambridge, Mass.: MIT Press, 1990), 49–72, 173–234; Nancy Stern, "John Von Neumann's Influence on Electronic Digital Computing, 1944–1946," *Annals of the History of Computing* 2, no. 4 (October 1980): 349–62.

35. Louis Couffignal, "Calcul mécanique: Sur l'emploi de la numeration binaire dans les machines a calculer et les instruments nomomécaniques," *Comptes Rendu du la Academie Scientifique Paris* 202 (1936): 1970–72; idem, "Sur

l'analyse mécanique. Application aux machines a calculer et aux calculs de la mécanique celeste," theses présentees a la Faculte des Sciences de Paris, ser. A (Paris: Gauthier-Villars, 1938); idem, "Sur un probleme d'analyse mécanique abstraite," *Comptes Rendu du la Academie Scientifique Paris* 206 (1938): 1336–38; and idem, "Sur une nouvelle machine a calculer," *Comptes Rendu du la Academie Scientifique Paris* 191 (1930): 924–26; Girolamo Ramunni, "Louis Couffignal, 1902–1966: Informatics Pioneer in France?" *Annals of the History of Computing* 11, no. 4 (1989): 247–56.

36. E. W. Phillips, "Binary Calculation," *Journal of the Institute of Actuaries* 67 (1936): 187–221; Emil L. Post, "Finite Combinatory Processes Formulation I," *Journal of Symbolic Logic* 1, no. 3 (1936): 103–5; R. L. A. Valtat, "Calcul mécanique: Machine a calculer fondee sur l'emploi de la numeration binaire," *Comptes Rendu du la Academie Scientifique Paris* 202 (1936): 1745–48; A. Weygandt, "Die elektromechanische DeterminantenOmaschine," *Zeit Instrumentenkde* 53 (1933): 114–21; C. E. Wynn-Williams, "Electrical Methods of Counting," *Reports Progressive Physics* 3 (1937): 239–61; and his recollections of work done in the 1930s, "The Scale of Two Counter," *Year Book Physics Society* (1957): 56–60.

37. J. F. Brennan, *The IBM Watson Laboratory at Columbia University: A History* (Armonk, N.Y.: IBM Corporation, 1971); W. J. Eckert, "The Role of the Punched Card in Scientific Computation," *Proceedings of the Industrial Computation Seminar,* September 1950 (New York: IBM Corporation, 1951), 13–17.

38. This work has been well summarized in John W. Stokes, *70 Years of Radio Tubes and Valves: A Guide for Electronic Engineers, Historians and Collectors* (Vestal, N.Y.: Vestal Press, 1982), with particular emphasis on the period between 1927 and 1937, which encompassed significant developments in tube technology.

39. "Complex Computer Demonstrated," *Bell Laboratories Record* 19, no. 2 (October 1940): v–vi; M. D. Fagen, ed., *A History of Engineering and Science in the Bell System: The Early Years (1875–1925)* (Murray Hill, N.J.: Bell Telephone Laboratories, 1975); and W. H. C. Higgins, B. D. Holbrook, "Defense Research at Bell Labs," *Annals of the History of Computing* 4, no. 3 (July 1982): 218–36, give a sense of early concerns.

40. H. L. Hazen et al., *The M.I.T. Network Analyzer* (Cambridge, Mass.: MIT Department of Electrical Engineering, April 1931); H. P. Kuehni and R. G. Lorraine, "A New A.C. Network Analyzer," *Transactions of the American Institute of Electrical Engineers* 57 (1938): 67–73; H. A. Peterson, "An Electric Circuit Transient Analyzer," *General Electric Review* (September 1939): 394–400. An analog computer is defined as a machine that computes "by manipulating continuous physical variables that are analogs of the quantities being subjected to computation," for example, voltage or time, *Dictionary of Computing* (Oxford: Oxford University Press, 1983), 12; a digital computer is defined as a machine that computes discrete quantities: "All computation is done within a finite number system and with limited precision, associated with the number of digits in the discrete numbers," *Dictionary of Computing,* 106. In other words, analog machines give approximate answers; digital devices provide exact numbers or data.

41. T. S. Gray, "A Photo-Electric Integraph," *Journal of the Franklin Institute*

212 (1931): 77–102; D. H. Lehmer, "A History of the Sieve Process," in Metropolis, Howlett, and Rota, *History of Computing,* 445–56.

42. C. E. Wynn-Williams, "A Thyratron 'Scale of Two' Automatic Counter," *Proceedings of the Royal Society of London,* ser. A, no. 136 (1932): 312–24; and his earlier article, "The Use of Thyratrons for High Speed Automatic Counting of Physical Phenomena," ibid., ser. A, no. 132 (1931): 295–310.

43. "Letter-Printing Cathode-Ray Tube," *Electronics* 22, no. 6 (June 1949): 160–62.

44. W. B. Lewis, "A 'Scale of Two' High-Speed Counter Using Hard Vacuum Triodes," *Proceedings of the Cambridge Philosophical Society* 33 (1937): 549–58; and his *Electrical Counting: With Special Reference to Alpha and Beta Particles* (London: Cambridge University Press, 1942); H. Lifschutz and J. L. Lawson, "A Triode Vacuum Tube Scale-of-Two Circuit," *Review of Scientific Instruments* 9 (March 1938): 83–89.

45. C. A. Beevers, "A Machine for the Rapid Summation of Fourier Series," *Proceedings of the Physical Society* 51, no. 4 (1939): 660–63.

46. C. E. Berry, "Design of Electrical Data Recording and Reading Mechanism" (Master's thesis, Iowa State College, Ames, 1941).

47. D. H. N. Caley, "Electricity and the 'Tote,'" *Electrician* 103, nos. 3–4 (July 19 and 26, 1929): 108–9.

48. L. J. Comrie, "Inverse Interpolation and Scientific Application of the National Accounting Machine," *Journal Royal Statistical Society,* suppl., 3, no. 2 (1936): 87–114, for example.

49. H. L. Hazen and G. S. Brown, "The Cinema Integraph, A Machine for Evaluating a Parametric Product Integral, With an Appendix by W. R. Hedeman, Jr.," *Journal of the Franklin Institute* 230 (1940): 19–44, 183–205.

50. H. L. Hazen et al., "The MIT Network Analyzer, Design and Application to Power System Problems," *Quarterly Transactions of the American Institute of Electrical Engineers* 49 (1930): 1102–14.

51. For example, see P. O. Crawford, Jr., "Instrumental Analysis in Matrix Algebra" (Bachelor's thesis, MIT, Cambridge, 1939); Karl L. Wildes and Nilo A. Lindgren, *A Century of Electrical Engineering and Computer Science at MIT, 1882–1982* (Cambridge, Mass.: MIT Press, 1985), 82–95.

52. J. Klir, "An Invention that Might Have Accelerated the Development of Mathematical Machines," *Technical Digest* 5, no. 5 (1963): 39–41.

53. D. M. Myers, "An Integraph for the Solution of Differential Equations of the Second Order," *Journal of Scientific Instruments* 16 (1939): 209–22.

54. C. L. Pekeris and W. T. White, "Differentiation with the Cinema Integraph," *Journal of the Franklin Institute* 234 (July 1942): 17–29.

Chapter 3

1. The most famous of the U.S. machines was made by E. G. Fischer and R. A. Harris for the U.S. Coast and Geodetic Survey to predict waves and completed in 1914 after fifteen years of work; see C. H. Claudy, "A Great Brass Brain," *Scientific American* 110 (March 7, 1914): 197–98; and R. A. Harris, "The Coast and Geodetic Survey Tide Predicting Machine," ibid. (June 13, 1914): 485. A

German version of the same machine was built at the Imperial Observatory in 1916, H. Rauschelbach, "Die Deutsche Gezeitenrechenmaschine," *Zeitschrift für Instrumentenkunde* 44 (July 1924): 285–303.

2. Michael R. Williams, *A History of Computing Technology* (Englewood Cliffs, N.J.: Prentice-Hall, 1985), 206–8.

3. He described his primary machine in Vannevar Bush, "The Differential Analyzer: A New Machine for Solving Equations," *Journal of the Franklin Institute* 212 (October 1931): 447–88. On his earlier work see H. L. Hazen with Vannevar Bush, "Integraph Solution of Differential Equations," ibid. 204 (1927): 575–615. For a historical overview see Larry Owens, "Vannevar Bush and the Differential Analyzer: The Text and Context of an Early Computer," *Technology and Culture* 27, no. 1 (January 1986): 63–95.

4. Robert L. Dietzold, "The Isograph—A Mechanical Root-Finder," *Bell Laboratories Record* 16, no. 4 (December 1937): 130–34.

5. H. C. Hart and Irven Travis, "Mechanical Solution of Algebraic Equations," *Journal of the Franklin Institute* 225 (January 1938): 63–72; D. L. Herr and R. S. Graham, "An Electrical Algebraic Equation Solver," *Review of Scientific Instruments* 9 (October 1938): 310–15.

6. R. O. Mercner, "The Mechanism of the Isograph," *Bell Laboratories Record* 16, no. 4 (December 1937): 135–40.

7. J. B. Wilbur, "The Mechanical Solution of Simultaneous Equations," *Journal of the Franklin Institute* 222 (December 1936): 715–24.

8. W. J. Duncan, "Some Devices for the Solution of Large Sets of Simultaneous Linear Equations," *Philosophical Magazine and Journal of Science* (London, Edinburgh, and Dublin) ser., 35, no. 7 (1944): 660–70; R. R. M. Mallock, "An Electrical Calculating Machine," *Proceedings of the Royal Society,* ser. A, 140 (1933): 457–83; James E. Tomayko, "Helmut Hoelzer's Fully Electronic Analog Computer," *Annals of the History of Computing* 7, no. 3 (July 1985): 227–40.

9. Owens, "Bush and the Differential Analyzer," 63–95.

10. Nancy Stern, *From ENIAC to UNIVAC: An Appraisal of the Eckert-Mauchly Computers* (Bedford, Mass.: Digital Press, 1981), 9–10.

11. Samuel H. Caldwell, "Educated Machinery," *Technology Review* 48, no. 1 (1945): 31–34; N. Genet, "100-Ton Brain at M.I.T.," *Scholastic* 48 (February 4, 1946): 36.

12. Karl L. Wildes and Nilo A. Lindgren, *A Century of Electrical Engineering and Computer Science at MIT, 1882–1982* (Cambridge, Mass.: MIT Press, 1985), 92.

13. Stern, *From ENIAC to UNIVAC,* 17.

14. "All the Answers at Your Fingertips: In the Laboratory of M.I.T.," *Popular Mechanics* 85 (March 1946): 16–167; "The Great Electro-Mechanical Brain: M.I.T.'s Differential Analyzer," *Life* 20 (January 14, 1946): 73–74; "M.I.T.'s 100-Ton Mathematical Brain Is Now to Tackle Problems of Peace," *Popular Science* 148 (January 1946): 81; "Robot Einstein: Differential Analyzer at M.I.T.," *Newsweek* 26 (November 12, 1945): 93.

15. Williams, *History of Computing Technology,* 213.

16. Ibid., for example, but see also Paul E. Ceruzzi, *Reckoners: The Prehistory of the Digital Computer, from Relays to the Stored Program Concept, 1935–1945* (Westport, Conn.: Greenwood Press, 1983); and an anthology written by

"pioneers" in N. Metropolis, J. Howlett, and Gian-Carlo Rota, eds., *A History of Computing in the Twentieth Century* (New York: Academic Press, 1980).

17. During the 1920s the average telephone user phoned some 200 times per year, by 1940, 250 times per year, and nearly 400 times per year by 1950. In 1920 there were approximately 105 telephones per 100,000 people in the United States, and over the period 1910–60 the number of telephones per 100,000 increased, on average, by 3.4 percent each year. For details on growth in dependence see John R. Pierce, "The Telephone and Society in the Past 100 Years," in Ithiel de Sola Pool, ed., *The Social Impact of the Telephone* (Cambridge, Mass.: MIT Press, 1977), 159–95.

18. M. G. Stevens, "Bell Labs: A Pioneer in Computing Technology," *Bell Laboratories Record* 51, no. 11 (1973): 344–51; George R. Stibitz, "Early Computers," in Metropolis, Howlett, and Rota, *History of Computing,* 479–83.

19. Williams, *History of Computing Technology,* 229–30.

20. O. Cesareo, "The Relay Interpolator," *Bell Laboratories Record* 23 (December 1946): 457–60; for an overview of all the models see Bernard D. Holbrook and W. Stanley Brown, *A History of Computing Research at Bell Laboratories (1937–1975),* Computing Science Technical Report no. 99 (Murray Hill, N.J.: Bell Telephone Laboratories, 1982).

21. E. G. Andrews, "A Review of Bell Laboratories Digital Computer Developments," *Proceedings of the Joint AIEE-IRE Computer Conference,* Philadelphia, December 10–12, 1951, passim; E. G. Andrews, "Telephone Switching and the Early Bell Laboratories Computers," *Bell System Technology Journal* 42 (1963): 341–53, reprinted in *Annals of the History of Computing* 4, no. 1 (January 1982): 13–19; F. M. Smits, ed., *A History of Engineering and Science in the Bell System: Electronics Technology (1925–1975)* (Indianapolis, Ind.: AT&T Bell Laboratories, 1985), gives a sense of working conditions and practices of the period; George R. Stibitz, "The Relay Computers at Bell Labs," *Datamation* 13, no. 4 (April 1967): 35–44, and ibid., no. 5 (May 1967): 45–49, are his memoirs.

22. Kenneth Flamm, *Creating the Computer: Government, Industry, and High Technology* (Washington, D.C.: Brookings Institution, 1988), 12–22, 29–79.

23. Charles J. Bashe, Lyle R. Johnson, and John H. Palmer, *IBM's Early Computers* (Cambridge, Mass.: MIT Press, 1986), 26–27.

24. Of the eighteen or so Ph.D. candidates trained by Aiken, the two most well-known graduates were An Wang, founder of Wang Laboratories, and Frederick P. Brooks, of IBM S/360 fame.

25. Bashe, Johnson, and Palmer, *IBM's Early Computers,* 31.

26. Ibid., 46. Watson commented, "In fact, the 603 was mainly a gimmick—it could calculate at electronic speeds, but that was not very useful because the punch cards couldn't keep up. But in spite of this, the thing caught on." Thomas J. Watson Jr. and Peter Petre, *Father Son & Co.: My Life at IBM and Beyond* (New York: Bantam, 1990), 137.

27. Quote is from Bashe, Johnson, and Palmer, *IBM's Early Computers,* 63; the general account is taken from ibid., 59–63.

28. Ibid.

29. Charles J. Bashe, "The SSEC in Historical Perspective," *Annals of the History of Computing* 4, no. 4 (October 1982): 296–312; John C. McPherson,

Frank E. Hamilton, and Robert R. Seeber, "A Large-Scale, General-Purpose Electronic Digital Calculator—The SSEC," ibid., 313–26.

30. Bashe, Johnson, and Palmer, *IBM's Early Computers*, 37–72. Watson provided his own statement about his interest in technology: "At that point I wasn't sure that building computers like the UNIVAC or abandoning punch cards for magnetic tape would ever make business sense." He thought computers still too clumsy and the technology not yet reliable enough; however, "I shared many of Dad's misgivings, but I was compelled by the tremendous speed of electronic circuits." Both quotes are from Watson, *Father Son & Co.*, 194. To keep informed he hired engineers, idem, Watson, *Father Son & Co.*, 196–97.

31. Bashe, Johnson, and Palmer, *IBM's Early Computers*, 14–15, 21–23, 61–62, 74–75, 89, and on the IBM 604, 59–68, 70–71, 73–74, 112–14, 316–17.

32. Michael S. Mahoney, "The History of Computing in the History of Technology," *Annals of the History of Computing* 10, no. 2 (1988): 115, 117.

33. Courses were taught, for example, at the Moore School in 1946, Stern, *From ENIAC to UNIVAC*, 92–96, while Aiken hosted conferences. For an example of the conference approach, see *Proceedings of a Symposium on Large-Scale Digital Calculating Machinery*, held at Harvard on January 7–10, 1947; reprint, Cambridge, Mass.: MIT Press, 1985.

34. Engineering Research Associates, Inc., *High-Speed Computing Devices* (New York: McGraw-Hill, 1950; reprint, Los Angeles, Calif.: Tomash Publishers, 1983), 165.

35. Williams, *History of Computing Technology*, 259.

36. Bashe, Johnson, and Palmer, *IBM's Early Computers*, 55–58, 130–36, 158–64.

37. Stern, *From ENIAC to UNIVAC*, 90–92.

38. Simon H. Lavington, *Early British Computers* (Maynard, Mass.: Digital Press, 1980), 8–12, 23–43.

39. Herman H. Goldstine, *The Computer from Pascal to Von Neumann* (Princeton, N.J.: Princeton University Press, 1972), 84–105, 127–236.

40. Stan Augarten, *Bit by Bit: An Illustrated History of Computers* (New York: Ticknor and Fields, 1984), 133–64, 188–223; Goldstine, *Computer from Pascal to Von Neumann*, 237–320; Williams, *History of Computing Technology*, 323–93; Metropolis, Howlett, and Rota, *History of Computing*.

41. Ceruzzi, *Reckoners*, 104–48; Flamm, *Creating the Computer*, 8–9, 25–26, 29–79; Bashe, Johnson, and Palmer, *IBM's Early Computers*; Stern, *From ENIAC to UNIVAC*, 1–5; Lavington, *Early British Computers*, 13–67.

42. This debate should not be confused with the patent controversy at the Moore School immediately after World War II that led Eckert and Mauchly to resign and to form their own company. For details see Stern, *From ENIAC to UNIVAC*, 53, 88–91.

43. Flamm, *Creating the Computer*, 8–9.

44. The concept of the computer revolution is defined not by the components of the machine but by how they were used, causing new ways of managing and thinking; Pamela McCorduck, *Machines Who Think* (San Francisco: W. H. Freeman, 1979), 48–49; Hiroshi Inose and John R. Pierce, *Information Technology and Civilization* (New York: W. H. Freeman, 1984), 105–23; Beniger argued that "the Control Revolution that eventually resulted was achieved by innovation at a

most fundamental level of technology—that of information processing and communication," in James R. Beniger, *The Control Revolution: Technological and Economic Origins of the Information Society* (Cambridge, Mass.: Harvard University Press, 1986), 287; Cohen also saw the impact of the computer as profound, perhaps revolutionary, I. Bernard Cohen, *Revolution in Science* (Cambridge, Mass.: Harvard University Press, 1985), 370.

45. E. W. Pugh, "Solid State Memory Development in IBM," *IBM Journal of Research and Development* 25, no. 5 (September 1981): 585–602; K. C. Smith and A. S. Sedra, "Memory," in Anthony Ralston and Edwin D. Reilly, Jr., eds., *Encyclopedia of Computer Science and Engineering* (New York: Van Nostrand Reinhold, 1983), 942–55.

46. Williams, *History of Computing Technology*, 304–23.

47. Ibid., 313–18.

48. Kent C. Redmond and Thomas M. Smith, *Project Whirlwind: The History of a Pioneer Computer* (Bedford, Mass.: Digital Press, 1980), 183–90, 206–7.

49. Ernest Braun and Stuart Macdonald, *Revolution in Miniature: The History and Impact of Semiconductor Electronics* (Cambridge: Cambridge University Press, 1982), 33–72.

50. S. Greenwald et al., "SEAC," *Proceedings, IRE* 41 (1953): 1300–13; U.S. Government, National Bureau of Standards, *Computer Development (SEAC and DYSEAC) at the National Bureau of Standards,* NBS Circular no. 551 (Washington, D.C.: U.S. Government Printing Office, 1955).

51. M. L. Lesser and J. W. Haanstra, "The Random-Access Memory Accounting Machine I. System Organization of the IBM 305," *IBM Journal of Research and Development* 1 (1957): 62–71; R. B. Mulvany and L. H. Thompson, "Innovations in Disk File Manufacturing," ibid. 25, no. 5 (September 1981): 711–23; M. E. Wolf, "The R&D Bootleggers: Inventing against the Odds," *IEEE Spectrum* 12 (1975): 38–45.

52. Bashe, Johnson, and Palmer, *IBM's Early Computers,* 273–314.

53. Montgomery Phister, Jr., *Data Processing Technology and Economics* (Santa Monica, Calif.: Santa Monica Publishing, 1976), on tape see 377–79, on disk see 368–75; Mulvany and Thompson, "Innovations in Disk File Manufacturing," 711–23; J. M. Harker et al., "A Quarter Century of Disk File Innovation," *IBM Journal of Research and Development* 25, no. 5 (September 1981): 677–89.

54. Jean E. Sammet, *Programming Languages: History and Fundamentals* (Englewood Cliffs, N.J.: Prentice-Hall, 1969), and idem, "Software History," in Anthony Ralston and Edwin D. Reilly, Jr., eds., *Encyclopedia of Computer Science and Engineering* (New York: Van Nostrand Reinhold, 1983), 1353–59.

55. Comments based on Sammet, *Progamming Languages,* passim; and L. Wexelblat, ed., *History of Programming Languages* (New York: Academic Press, 1981), passim.

56. Norman Weizer, "A History of Operating Systems," *Datamation* (January 1981): 119–20, 125–26; James W. Cortada, *Historical Dictionary of Data Processing: Technology* (Westport, Conn.: Greenwood Press, 1987), 279–93.

57. Bashe, Johnson, and Palmer, *IBM's Early Computers,* 34–186.

58. Franklin M. Fisher, James W. McKie, and Richard B. Mancke, *IBM and the U.S. Data Processing Industry: An Economic History* (New York: Praeger, 1983), 3–26.

59. Ceruzzi, *Reckoners,* 127–28.

60. Bashe, Johnson, and Palmer, *IBM's Early Computers,* for a detailed account, machine-by-machine of the process in some seven hundred pages.

61. Lavington, *Early British Computers,* 12, 23.

62. Ibid., 31–35; Maurice Wilkes, *Memoirs of a Computer Pioneer* (Cambridge, Mass.: MIT Press, 1985), 127–42.

63. Lavington, *Early British Computers,* 23–25, 27–30, 36–42, 48–52.

64. Goldstine, *Computer from Pascal to Von Neumann,* 204–70.

65. Knowledge on French activities recently grew with the dedication of an entire issue of the *Annals of the History of Computing* to the subject. Key articles include Pierre E. Mounier-Kuhn, "Prologue: History of Computing in France," *Annals of the History of Computing* 11, no. 4 (1989): 237–40; and idem,"Bull: A World-Wide Company Born in Europe," ibid., 279–97; Jacques Vernay, "IBM France," ibid., 299–311. The *Annals* also announced in the same issue that it would publish future numbers dedicated to countries in Europe to address the lack of details on the subject.

66. William Aspray, "International Diffusion of Computer Technology, 1945–1955," *Annals of the History of Computing* 8, no. 3 (1986): 351–60.

67. Too much attention has been paid by historians and writers of the history of computing to who first invented the digital computer. The literature on the subject continues to grow. For a pro-Mauchly view see Nancy Stern, "Who Invented the First Electronic Digital Computer?" *Abacus* 1, no. 1 (1983): 7–15; and for an opposing view, John Vincent Atanasoff, "Advent of Electronic Digital Computing," *Annals of the History of Computing* 6, no. 3 (July 1984): 229–82.

68. Goldstine, *Computer from Pascal to Von Neumann,* 149.

69. Ibid., 148–56.

70. Ibid., 182; Nancy Stern, "John Von Neumann's Influence on Electronic Digital Computing, 1944–1946," *Annals of the History of Computing* 2, no. 4 (October 1980): 349–62.

71. Goldstine, *Computer from Pascal to Von Neumann,* 211–24.

72. Ibid., 211.

73. Ibid., 217.

74. Wilkes, *Memoirs of a Computer Pioneer,* 14, 119–21.

75. Goldstine, *Computer from Pascal to Von Neumann,* 217.

76. Ibid., 219–20.

77. Maurice Wilkes, David J. Wheeler, and Stanley Gill, *The Preparation of Programs for an Electronic Digital Computer, with Special Reference to the EDSAC and the Use of Library Subroutines* (Cambridge, Mass.: Addison-Wesley, 1951; reprint, Los Angeles, Calif.: Tomash Publishers, 1982), preface.

78. The Staff of the Computation Laboratory, *A Manual of Operation for the Automatic Sequence Controlled Calculator* (Cambridge, Mass.: Harvard University Press, 1946; reprint, Cambridge, Mass.: MIT Press, 1985).

79. The proceedings were published as *Proceedings of a Symposium on Large-Scale Digital Calculating Machinery* (Cambridge, Mass.: Harvard University Press, 1948; reprint, William Aspray, ed., Cambridge, Mass.: MIT Press, 1985); the figure of one thousand was drawn from Aspray's introduction to the reprint, ix.

80. Ibid. reprint, ix–x.

81. I. L. Auerbach, "Association for Computing Machinery (CSM)," in An-

thony Ralston and Chester L. Meeks, eds., *Encyclopedia of Computer Science* (New York: Petrocelli/Charter, 1976), 128–29.

82. Aspray, *Proceedings of a Symposium,* xi–xix.

83. Ibid., xxi–xxiii.

84. Ibid., x.

85. Wilkes, *Memoirs of a Computer Pioneer,* 144–45.

86. Aspray, *Proceedings of a Symposium,* x.

87. Greater organization and codification is demonstrated by the demand for such publications as *Engineering Research Associates, Inc., High Speed Computing Devices* (New York: McGraw-Hill, 1950; reprint, Los Angeles, Calif.: Tomash Publishers, 1983). On organizations see individual histories in Cortada, *Historical Dictionary of Data Processing: Organizations* (Westport, Conn.: Greenwood Press, 1987): ASIS, 51–52, ACM, 64–65, ASM, 66–67, DPMA, 111–12, GUIDE, 137–38, IEEE, 155, IFIP, 173–74, SHARE, 245–46, SCS, 246–47.

88. *Communications of the ACM.*

89. An Wang, *Lessons: An Autobiography* (Reading, Mass.: Addison-Wesley, 1986), 46.

90. Ibid., 46–47.

91. Ibid., 47.

92. Wilkes, *Memoirs of a Computer Pioneer,* 123.

93. Ibid., 120.

94. Ibid., 127.

95. Ibid., 139.

96. Ibid., 143.

97. Stern, *From ENIAC to UNIVAC,* 95.

98. Ibid., 93–95.

99. Herman Lukoff, *From Dits to Bits: A Personal History of the Electronic Computer* (Portland, Ore.: Robotics Press, 1979), 60.

100. Ibid., 69.

101. Ibid., 70.

102. John Backus, "Programming in America in the 1950s Some Personal Impressions," in Metropolis, Howlett, and Rota, *History of Computing,* 126–27.

103. Ibid., 127.

104. Julian Bigelow, "Computer Development at the Institute for Advanced Study," Metropolis, Howlett, and Rota, *History of Computing,* 294.

105. Ibid., 291–310.

106. Robert R. Everett, "Whirlwind," in Metropolis, Howlett, and Rota, *History of Computing,* 366.

107. See, for example, Redmond and Smith, *Project Whirlwind,* 196.

108. Flamm, *Creating the Computer,* 69, 74–75.

109. Edwin Tomash, "The Start of an ERA: Engineering Research Associates, Inc., 1946–1955," in Metropolis, Howlett, and Rota, *History of Computing,* 485–95.

110. Paul Freiberger and Michael Swaine, *Fire in the Valley: The Making of the Personal Computer* (Berkeley, Calif.: Osborne/McGraw-Hill, 1984), 216–20.

111. The classic statement is by Frederick P. Brooks, Jr., *The Mythical Man-Month: Essays on Software Engineering* (Reading, Mass.: Addison-Wesley, 1975); for case studies, Susan Lammers, ed., *Programmers at Work* (Redmond, Wash.: Microsoft Press, 1986).

Chapter 4

1. They can be good histories nonetheless. See, for example, Charles J. Bashe, Lyle R. Johnson, and John H. Palmer, *IBM's Early Computers* (Cambridge, Mass.: MIT Press, 1986); or N. Metropolis, J. Howlett, and Gian-Carlo Rota, eds., *A History of Computing in the Twentieth Century* (New York: Academic Press, 1980).

2. J. Delmont, "ERA: Control Data's Forerunner in a Gloomy Glider Factory," *Contact* (July 1976): 3–6; Erwin Tomash, "The Start of an ERA: Engineering Research Associates, Inc., 1946–1955," in Metropolis, Howlett, and Rota, *History of Computing*, 485–95.

3. Franklin M. Fisher, James W. McKie, and Richard B. Mancke, *IBM and the U.S. Data Processing Industry: An Economic History* (New York: Praeger, 1983), 26–46, for the best example of this interpretation.

4. William W. Simmons with Richard B. Elsberry, *Inside IBM: The Watson Years* (Bryn Mawr, Pa.: Dorrance, 1988), 70–71.

5. Kenneth Flamm, *Creating the Computer: Government, Industry, and High Technology* (Washington, D.C.: Brookings Institution, 1988), 12–21, 29–79.

6. Ibid., 16.

7. Ibid., 18, references data from U.S. Department of Commerce, Industry and Trade Administration Office of Producer Goods, *A Report on the U.S. Semiconductor Industry* (Washington, D.C.: U.S. Government Printing Office, 1979), 8.

8. Flamm, *Creating the Computer*, 25–26; for the panel selection of languages, see L. Wexelblat, ed., *History of Programming Languages* (New York: Academic Press, 1981), which is a collection of essays on each one.

9. Flamm, *Creating the Computer*, 29.

10. Ibid., 16.

11. On the IBM 701 and IBM 702 see Bashe, Johnson, and Palmer, *IBM's Early Computers*, 130–47, 158–64, 173–78; on the UNIVAC see Nancy Stern, *From ENIAC to UNIVAC: An Appraisal of the Eckert-Mauchly Computers* (Bedford, Mass.: Digital Press, 1981), 7–23.

12. Flamm, *Creating the Computer*, 78.

13. Ibid.

14. Ibid., 79.

15. Flamm, *Creating the Computer*, 46; and, also, for my account of ERA see James W. Cortada, *Historical Dictionary of Data Processing: Organizations* (Westport, Conn.: Greenwood Press, 1987), 43–46; see also, Fisher, McKie, and Mancke, *IBM and the U.S. Data Processing Industry*, 6, 9–10.

16. Flamm, *Creating the Computer*, 65.

17. Ibid., 67.

18. Ibid., 67–68.

19. Marie Anchordoguy, *Computers Inc.: Japan's Challenge to IBM* (Cambridge, Mass.: Council on East Asian Studies, Harvard University, 1989), 19–92.

20. Flamm, *Creating the Computer*, 12–45.

21. Anchordoguy, *Computers Inc.*, 36.

22. Ibid., 53.

23. Ibid., 167.

York: Ticknor and Fields, 1984), 218–19; Sobel, *IBM*, 148, 150–52, are examples.

78. Flamm, *Creating the Computer*, 83–86.

79. Ibid., 82.

80. Ibid., 80–107.

81. Fisher, McKie, and Mancke, *IBM and the U.S. Data Processing Industry*, 7.

82. In fact, however, the British EDSAC was probably the first; Maurice Wilkes, David J. Wheeler, and Stanley Gill, *Memoirs of a Computer Pioneer* (Cambridge, Mass.: MIT Press, 1985), 143–53, 191–93.

83. Stern, *From ENIAC to UNIVAC*, 105–6.

84. Herbert F. Mitchell, Jr., "Electronic Computers in Inventory Control," *Proceedings of the Conference on Operations Research in Production and Inventory Control*, January 20–22, 1954 (Cleveland, Ohio: Case Institute of Technology, 1954), 61–67; and the most important of the early articles on GE's use of UNIVAC I, Roddy F. Osborn, "GE and UNIVAC: Harnessing the High-Speed Computer," *Harvard Business Review* 32, no. 4 (July–August 1954): 99–107. The vendor published a formal application brief, *Remington Rand, The General Electric Company Sales Analysis Application* (New York: Remington Rand Univac, 1957), 24 pages. Other publicity for the initial commercial Univac included G. M. Sheean, "A Univac Progress Report," *Systems* 20 (March–April 1956): 334; Julius Shiskin, "Seasonal Computations on Univac," *American Statistician* 9 (February 1955): 19–23.

85. For a good summary see Flamm, *Creating the Computer*, 43–46.

86. Fisher, McKie, and Mancke, *IBM and the U.S. Data Processing Industry*, 9.

87. Ibid., 10.

88. Ibid., 39.

89. Ibid.

90. Ibid., 40.

91. Simmons and Elsberry, *Inside IBM*, 124–30.

92. Fisher, McKie, and Mancke, *IBM and the U.S. Data Processing Industry*, 41.

93. David E. Lundstrom, *A Few Good Men from Univac* (Cambridge, Mass.: MIT Press, 1987): 36, 45–46, also addressed the lack of management efficiency and commitment to Univac.

94. Ibid. for a memoir of the early days at CDC; Donna Raimondi, "From Code Busters to Mainframes. The History of CDC," *ComputerWorld*, July 15, 1985, pp. 93, 98–99.

95. Fisher, McKie, and Mancke, *IBM and the U.S. Data Processing Industry*, 40.

96. Ibid., 45–46.

97. *Business Week*, November 22, 1969, cited in ibid., 474.

98. W. N. de Bruijn, *Computers in Europe, 1966* (Amsterdam, Netherlands: Automatic Information Processing Research Center, 1966) relates the story by country from 1955; J. Connolly, *History of Computing in Europe* (New York: IBM World Trade Corporation, 1967), remains a treasure of detail on computing in the 1950s; Jacques and Jean-Michel Quatrepoint Jublin, *French Ordinateurs de l'affaire Bull a l'assassinat du Plan Calcul* (Paris: Editions Alain Moreau, 1976), has material dating back to the 1950s; H. R. Schwartz, "The Early Years of Computing in Switzerland," *Annals of the History of Computing* 3, no. 2 (April 1981): 121–32; and on German issues see Vladimir Stibic, *Wege von der Mechanisierung zur Automatisierung der Verwaltungsarbeit* (Berlin: Verlag Die

Wirtschaft, 1962); Alwin Walther, "German Computing," *Datamation* 6 (September 1960): 27ff. On Eastern Europe and the Soviet Union, see R. W. Marczynski, "The First Seven Years of Polish Digital Computers," *Annals of the History of Computing* 2, no. 1 (January 1980): 37–48; William Keith McHenry, "The Absorption of Computerized Management Information Systems in Soviet Enterprises" (Ph.D. diss., University of Arizona, Tucson, 1985); Jan G. Oblonsky, "The Development of the Research Institute of Mathematical Machines in Prague," *Information Processing Machines* 10 (1964): 15–24; reprint, *Annals of the History of Computing* 2, no. 4 (October 1980): 294–98.

99. Very few surveys exist. Of some use are Computer Consultants, Ltd., *European Computer Survey* (London: Pergamon Press, 1968), on the 1960s; Council of Europe, *The Computer Industry in Europe: Hardware Manufacturing,* Doc. 2893, (1971); Giovanni Dosi, *Industrial Adjustment and Policy: II; Technical Change and Survival: Europe's Semiconductor Industry* (Brighton, U.K.: Sussex European Research Center, 1981); European Economic Community, *L'Industrie électronique des pays de la communauté et les investissements Americains (Collection Etudes),* Serie Industrie, no. 1 (Brussels: European Economic Community, 1969); Y. S. Hu, *The Impact of U.S. Investment in Europe: A Case Study of the Automotive and Computer Industries* (New York: Praeger, 1973); Nicolas Jequier, "Computers," in Raymond Vernon, ed., *Big Business and the State: Changing Relations in Western Europe* (Cambridge, Mass.: Harvard University Press, 1974), 195–228; Wayne J. Lee, *The International Computer Industry* (Washington, D.C.: Applied Library Resources, Inc., 1971).

100. New information on European conditions is appearing. See Martin Cambell-Kelly, *ICL: A Business and Technical History* (Oxford: Oxford University Press, 1989); for France, see the entire issue of *Annals of the History of Computing* 11, no. 4 (1989).

101. David S. Landes, *The Unbound Prometheus: Technological Change and Industrial Development in Western Europe from 1750 to the Present* (Cambridge: Cambridge University Press, 1969), 495–98.

102. Flamm, *Targeting the Computer,* 153–72.

103. Pierre E. Mounier-Kuhn, "Bull: A World-Wide Company Born in Europe," *Annals of the History of Computing* 11, no. 4 (1989): 279–97.

104. Flamm, *Creating the Computer,* 148–49.

105. Ibid., 135.

106. Ibid.

107. Lavington, *Early British Computers,* 78.

108. Ibid., but see also Flamm, *Creating the Computer.*

109. Lavington, *Early British Computers,* 78.

110. John Hendry, "The Teashop Computer Manufacturer: J. Lyons, Leo and the Potentials and Limits of High-Tech Diversification," *Business History* 29 (1987): 66–72.

111. Flamm, *Creating the Computer,* 146–47.

112. Ibid., 151–52.

113. Ibid.; Henri François-Henri Raymond, "An Adventure with a Sad Ending: The SEA," *Annals of the History of Computing* 11, no. 4 (1989): 263–77.

114. A. P. Speiser, "The Relay Calculator Z4," *Annals of the History of Computing* 2, no. 3 (July 1980): 242–45; Konrad Zuse, "Die ersten programmgesteuerten

Relais-Rechenmaschinen," in M. Graef, ed., *350 Jahre Rechenmaschinen* (Munich: Carl Hanser, 1973), 51–57; and his memoirs, *Der Computer—Mein Lebenswerk* (Munich: Verlag Moderne Industrie, 1970).

115. Because the R&D for the IBM 650 had been funded by military and commercial demand in the U.S., IBM could introduce it in Europe at no cost other than for the actual assemblage of the system, transportation, and marketing. Its European competitors had to carry the burden of R&D expense and manufacturing costs at a lower level of experience while competing against advanced technology and a well-managed rival. For details of IBM's role in Europe see Nancy Foy, *The Sun Never Sets on IBM* (New York: William Morrow, 1975), 55–56ff. Selling in Europe can be understood better through the memoirs of an IBM marketing executive than a sales representative; Jacques Maisonrouge, *Inside IBM: A Personal Story* (New York: McGraw-Hill, 1988), 65–92.

116. Flamm, *Creating the Computer,* 160–61; Everett S. Calhoun, "New Computer Developments around the World," in *1956 Proceedings of the Eastern Joint Computer Conference* (New York: American Institute of Electrical Engineers, 1957), 6–7; Friedrich L. Bauer, "Between Zuse and Rutishauser," in Metropolis, Howlett, and Rota, *History of Computing,* 517.

117. But see Connolly, *History of Computing in Europe;* "Datamation's International Computer Census," *Datamation* 8, no. 8 (August 1962): 46–48.

118. Flamm, *Creating the Computer,* 166.

119. Ibid., 166–71.

120. Ibid.

Chapter 5

1. A good example of an important document that first circulated in an unpublished form was John Von Neumann's "First Draft of a Report on the EDVAC," written in 1945 and published in full for the first time in 1981 in Nancy Stern, *From ENIAC to UNIVAC: An Appraisal of the Eckert-Mauchly Computers* (Bedford, Mass.: Digital Press, 1981), 179–246.

2. "Quiz Robot Solves Motion Problems; Apparatus Called a Mechanical Transient Analyzer," *Science Digest* 18 (October 1945): 96; "Mathematical Machine; New Electronic Differential Analyzer," *Science News Letter* 48 (November 10, 1945): 291.

3. N. Genet, "100-Ton Brain at Massachusetts Institute of Technology," *Senior Scholastic* 48 (February 4, 1946): 36; "Oil Field Fortune Teller; Electronic Oil Pool Analyzer," *Popular Mechanics* 86 (September 1946): 154; A. Rose, "Lightning Strikes Mathematics: ENIAC," ibid. 85 (April 1946): 8–86; "It Thinks with Electrons: The ENIAC," ibid. 85 (June 1946): 139; "M.I.T.'s 100-Ton Mathematical Brain Is Now to Tackle Problems of Peace," *Popular Science* 148 (January 1946): 81; "Electronic Calculator: ENIAC," *Scientific American* 174 (June 1946): 248; "Calculators," *Science Illustrated* 1 (May 1946): 70–72.

4. "Tube with a Memory: RCA's Selectron," *Popular Science* 150 (June 1947): 144; S. L. Freeland, "Inside the Biggest Man-Made Brain: Navy's New Calculator," ibid., 150 (May 1947): 95–100; J. Markus, "Predictions by Electronics; Oil-Pool Analyzer," *Scientific American* 176 (May 1947): 207–9; "Math Data

Can Be Kept Permanently by New Device," *Science News Letter* 52. (November 15, 1947): 313; "Machines Speed Science," *Science News Letter* 51 (January 25, 1947): 51–52; "Electronic Computer Faster than ENIAC to Be Developed," ibid. 51 (February 8, 1947): 83; "EDVAC II to Calculate Census for Government," ibid. 51 (March 22, 1947): 184.

5. "Robot Einstein; Differential Analyzer at the Massachusetts Institute of Technology," *Newsweek* 26 (November 12, 1945): 93; "New Robot Calculates Dividends and Writes Checks," *Business Week,* July 14, 1945, 70; for example, from 1946: "Robot Calculator; ENIAC, All-Electronic Device," *Business Week,* February 16, 1946, 50ff.; "Answers by ENY; Electronic Numerical Integrator and Computer, ENIAC," *Newsweek* 27 (February 18, 1946): 76; "ENIAC: At the University of Pennsylvania," *Time* 47 (February 25, 1946): 90; "Great Electro-Mechanical Brain; M.I.T.'s Differential Analyzer," *Life* 20 (January 14, 1946): 73–74ff.

6. "Machines Predict What Happens in Your Plant; Instruments Guide Industry; The Analog," *Business Week,* September 25, 1948, 68ff.; "Electronic War Production Board; Electronic Computer," ibid. (October 9, 1948): 22–24; "Business Predictor, Univac," ibid. (June 5, 1948): 75; "Third-R Machine; Selective Sequence Electronic Calculator," *Newsweek* 31 (February 9, 1948): 43; "Horses and Calculus; Reeves Electronic Analogue Computer," ibid. 31 (June 14, 1948): 54–55; "For Sale: Electronic Brains; Eckert-Mauchly Computer Corp.," ibid. 31 (April 5, 1948): 53; H. H. Adise, "Office-Size Electronic Calculator," *Aviation Week* 49 (July 26, 1948): 18ff.; "Memory on Film," *Science Digest* 23 (February 1948): 70–71; "Cybernetics, New Science; In Man's Image," *Time* 52 (December 27, 1948): 45; W. J. Eckert, "Electrons and Computation," *Scientific Monthly* 67 (November 1948): 315–23.

7. Sidney Ratner et al., *The Evolution of the American Economy: Growth, Welfare, and Decision Making* (New York: Basic Books, 1979): 404–6.

8. William Aspray and Donald deB. Beaver, "Marketing the Monster: Advertising Computer Technology," *Annals of the History of Computing* 8, no. 2 (April 1986): 127–43.

9. Ibid., quote on page 130.

10. Ibid., 131.

11. Ibid., 133.

12. Ralph W. Fairbanks, "Electronics in the Modern Office," *Harvard Business Review* 30, no. 5 (September–October 1952): 83–98, the first article in *HBR* on the commercial uses of the computer; John Diebold, "Automation: The New Technology," ibid., 32, no. 6 (November–December 1953): 63–71; Cyril C. Hermann, "Operations Research for Management," ibid. 32, no. 4 (July–August 1953): 100–112; John A. Higgins and Joseph S. Glickauf, "Electronics Down to Earth," ibid. 32, no. 3 (March–April 1954): 97–104; Roddy F. Osborn, "GE and UNIVAC: Harnessing the High-Speed Computer," ibid. 32, no. 4 (July–August 1954): 99–107; Richard F. Clippinger, "Economics of the Digital Computer," ibid. 33, no. 1 (January–February 1955): 77–88; M. L. Hurni, "Decision Making in the Age of Automation," ibid. 34, no. 5 (September–October 1955): 49–58.

13. For example, Haskell B. Curry and Willa A. Wyatt, "A Study of Inverse Interpolation of the Eniac," B.R.L. Report no. 615 (Aberdeen, Md.: Ballistic Research Laboratories, August 19, 1946); S. Gill, "A Process for the Step-by-Step

Integration of Differential Equations in an Automatic Digital Computing Machine," *Proceedings of the Cambridge Philosophical Society* 47 (1951): 9–108; Dorrit Hoffleit, "A Comparison of Various Computing Machines Used in Reduction of Doppler Observations," *Mathematical Tables and Other Aids to Computation* 3, no. 25 (January 1949): 373–77; Herbert F. Mitchell, Jr., "Inversion of a Matrix of Order 38," *Mathematical Tables and Other Aids to Computation* 3, no. 3 (July 1948): 161–66; even in the trade press: "Weather under Control," *Fortune*, February 1948, 106–11ff.

14. George E. Kimball and Philip M. Morse, *Methods of Operations Research* (New York: John Wiley, 1951); Joseph F. McCoskey and Florence N. Trefethen, eds., *Operations Research for Management* (Baltimore: Johns Hopkins Press, 1954), see for early history, 3–35.

15. Adolph H. Matz, "Electronics in Accounting," *Accounting Review* 21, no. 4 (October 1946): 371–79.

16. American Association of Collegiate Registrars and Admissions Officers, Committee on Machine Equipment, *Office Machine Equipment* (Chicago: American Association of Collegiate Registrars and Admissions Officers, 1959); for summary of work done in the 1950s by the AMA see American Management Association, *Data Processing Today: A Progress Report* (New York: AMA, 1960); U.S. Congress, *Hearings before the Subcommittee on the Economic Stabilization of the Joint Committee on the Economic Report, Automation and Technological Change*, 84th Cong., 1st sess. (Washington, D.C.: U.S. Government Printing Office, 1955); Bank Management Commission, *Automation of Bank Operating Procedures* (New York: American Bankers Association, 1955); Proceedings of the Eastern Joint Computer Conference, *Computers with Deadlines to Meet* (New York: Institute of Radio Engineers, 1958); General Electric Company, *The Next Step in Management: An Appraisal of Cybernetics* (New York: General Electric, 1952); Herbert F. Klingman, ed., *Electronics in Business* (New York: Controllership Foundation, 1955), has an extensive bibliography on business applications, seminars and classes, and a list of major data centers; Report Committee, Society of Actuaries, *A New Recording: Means and Computing Services* (Chicago: Society of Actuaries, 1952).

17. Arthur A. Brown and Leslie G. Peck, "How Electronic Machines Handle Clerical Work," *Journal of Accountancy* 99 (January 1955): 31–37; Everett S. Calhoun, *The Challenge of Electronic Equipment to Accountants* (Stanford, Calif.: Stanford Research Institute, 1953), a thirteen-page booklet; Dorothy Colburn, "The Computer as an Accountant," *Automatic Control* 1 (December 1954): 19–21.

18. Bernard S. Benson, "Cut Research and Development Costs," *Automatic Control* 3 (October 1955): 22–26; John F. Bishop, "Analogue or Digital Control?" ibid. 1 (December 1954): 16–18; R. G. Canning, "Cost Reduction through Electronic Production Control," *Mechanical Engineering* 75 (November 1953): 887–90; Lawrence P. Lassing, "Computers in Business," *Scientific American* 190 (January 1954): 21–25; M. E. Salveson and R. G. Canning, "Automatic Data Processing in Larger Manufacturing Plants," in *Proceedings of the Western Computer Conference* (New York: Institute of Radio Engineers, 1953), 65–73; C. W. Schmidt and R. Bosak, "Production Scheduling and Labor Budgeting with Computers," in *Electronic Data Processing in Industry: A Casebook of Management*

Experience (New York: American Management Association, 1955), 206–14.

19. Robert W. Burgess, *"Statement . . ." Automation and Technological Change,* 78–82; and on early activities see Nick A. Komons, *Science and the Air Force: A History of the Air Force Office of Scientific Research* (Arlington, Va.: Historical Division, Office of Information, U.S. Air Force, 1966); and David F. Noble, *Forces of Production: A Social History of Industrial Automation* (New York: Alfred Knopf, 1984).

20. A. V. Astin, *"Statement . . ." Automation and Technological Change,* 571–89; Derrick H. Lehmer et al., "An Application of High-Speed Computing to Fermat's Last Theorem," *Proceedings, National Academy of Science, USA* 40 (1954): 25–33; W. W. Piper and J. S. Prener, "Hartree-Fock Wave Functions for MN," *Physical Review* 100 (1955): 1250; see also Bonnie Kaplan, "Computers in Medicine, 1950–1980: The Relationship between History and Policy," (Ph.D. diss., University of Chicago, 1984).

21. For a contemporary bibliography of other publications, see General Electric Company, *Next Step in Management,* 181–82.

22. American Management Association, *Electronics in the Office: Problems and Prospects* (New York: American Management Association, 1952); American Management Association, *A New Approach to Office Mechanization* (New York: American Management Association, 1954); American Management Association, *The Impact of Computers on Office Management* (New York: American Management Association, 1954); "Office Automation," *Dun's Review and Modern Industry* (October 1955): 54–114.

23. U.S. Department of Labor, Bureau of Labor Statistics, *Automation and Employment Opportunities for Office Workers,* Occupational Outlook Series, Bulletin no. 1241 (Washington, D.C.: U.S. Government Printing Office, 1958); and idem, *Adjustments to the Introduction of Office Automation,* Bulletin no. 1276 (Washington, D.C.: U.S. Government Printing Office, May 1960).

24. R. Hunt Brown, *Office Automation* (New York: Automation Consultant, Inc., 1955).

25. Robert N. Anthony and Samuel Schwartz, *Office Equipment: Buy or Rent?* (Boston: Management Analysis Center, 1957); Richard G. Canning, *Electronic Data Processing for Business and Industry* (New York: John Wiley, 1956); Ned Chapin, *An Introduction to Automatic Computers* (New York: D. Van Nostrand, 1955); Harold F. Craig, *Administering a Conversion to Electronic Accounting* (Boston: Harvard University, Graduate School of Business Administration, 1955); Robert H. Gregory and Richard L. Van Horn, *Automatic Data-Processing Systems: Principles and Procedures* (San Francisco: Wadsworth Publishing, 1960); Leon C. Guest, "Administrative Automation at Sylvania: A Case Study—I. Centralized Data Processing—Decentralized Management," in *Administrative Automation through IDP and EDP,* Office Management Series no. 144 (New York: American Management Association, 1956), 28–37; Lowell H. Hattery and George P. Bush, eds., *Electronics in Management* (Washington, D.C.: University Press, 1956); Peter B. Laubach, *Company Investigations of Automatic Data Processing* (Boston: Harvard University, Graduate School of Business Administration, 1957); Myron B. Solo, "Selecting Electronic Data Processing Equipment," *Datamation* (November–December 1958): 28–32; William H. Starbuck, "Computing Machines: Rent or Buy?" *Journal of Industrial Engineering* 9, no. 4 (July–August 1958): 254–58.

26. Frank Wallace, *Appraising the Economics of Electronic Computers* (New York: Controllership Foundation, 1956).

27. There were exceptions, of course; see, for example, C. E. Weber, "Change in Managerial Manpower with Mechanization of Data-Processing," *Journal of Business* 32, no. 2 (April 1959): 151–63.

28. Franklin M. Fisher, James W. McKie, and Richard B. Mancke, *IBM and the U.S. Data Processing Industry: An Economic History* (New York: Praeger, 1983), 19–20.

29. Ibid., 22.

30. William W. Simmons and Richard B. Elsberry, *Inside IBM: The Watson Years* (Bryn Mawr, Pa.: Dorrance, 1988), 124–30.

31. The best of these articles was Roddy F. Osborn, "GE and UNIVAC," 99–107, which summarizes some of the publicity.

32. General Electric Company, *Next Step in Management,* vii.

33. Ibid., 73–74.

34. Ibid., 91–95.

35. Ibid., 103–4.

36. Ibid., 105.

37. Ibid., 176.

38. Fisher, McKie, and Mancke, *IBM and the U.S. Data Processing Industry,* 4–5.

39. Richard G. Canning, *Electronic Data Processing for Business and Industry* (New York: John Wiley, 1956), 137.

40. Adam Abruzzi, "The Power of Automation," *Automation* 3, no. 12 (December 1956): 38–42; Ned Chapin, "Justifying the Use of an Automatic Computer," *Journal of Machine Accounting, Systems and Management* 6, no. 8 (September 1955): 9–10, 14; R. D. Dotts, "An Approach to Electronics by a Medium Sized Company," *Journal of Machine Accounting, Systems and Management* 5, no. 11 (December 1954): 8–9. I am studying this category of articles for a book I am writing about how computers have been used in a commercial environment. I intend to publish simultaneously a book-length bibliographic guide to this large body of literature.

41. Harold J. Leavitt and Thomas J. Whisler, "Management in the 1980s," *Harvard Business Review* 36, no. 6 (November–December 1958): 41–48.

42. James D. Gallagher, *Improving the Organization and Management of the Data-Processing Function* (New York: American Management Association, 1960).

43. For example, L. Fred Boyce, Jr., "Installing a Medium-Sized Computer," *Journal of Accountancy* 110 (July 1960): 48–53; Robert E. Schlosser, "System Mechanization and the Small Practitioner," *Journal of Accountancy* 108 (November 1959): 51–54.

44. John Diebold, "Automation, 1958: Industry at the Crossroads," *Dun's Review and Modern Industry* (August 1958): 36–39.

45. Ibid., 37.

46. For example, Pamela Haddy, "Some Thoughts on Automation in a British Office," *Journal of Industrial Economics* 6, no. 2 (February 1958): 161–70.

47. For details see James W. Cortada, ed., *Archives of Data-Processing History: A Guide to Major U.S. Collections* (Westport, Conn.: Greenwood Press, 1990), 51–72, 121–28, 129–40.

48. Kenneth Flamm, *Creating the Computer: Government, Industry, and High Technology* (Washington, D.C.: Brookings Institution, 1988) 82.

49. Ibid., 135.

50. Montgomery Phister, Jr., *Data Processing Technology and Economics* (Santa Monica, Calif.: Santa Monica Publishing, 1976), 243.

51. Ibid., 240.

52. Ibid., 20.

53. Ibid., 25.

54. Ibid., 277.

55. Ibid., 42–43.

56. Ibid., 323.

57. John E. Tilton, *International Diffusion of Technology: The Case of Semiconductors* (Washington, D.C.: Brookings Institution, 1971); A. Horsley and G. M. P. Swann, "A Time Series of Computer Price Functions," *Oxford Bulletin of Economics and Statistics* 45 (November 1983): 339–56; Ellen R. Dulberger, "The Application of a Hedonic Model to a Quality-Adjusted Price Index for Computer Processors," in Dale W. Jorgenson and Ralph Landau, eds., *Technology and Capital Formation* (Cambridge, Mass: MIT Press, 1989), 37–75; Robert B. Archibald and William S. Reece, "Partial Subindexes of Input Prices: The Case of Computer Services," *Southern Economic Journal* 46 (October 1979): 528–40; David W. Cartwright, "Improved Deflation of Purchases of Computer," *Survey of Current Business* (March 1986): 7–9; Rosanne Cole et al., "Quality-Adjusted Price Indexes for Computer Processors and Selected Peripheral Equipment," *Survey of Current Business* (January 1986): 41–50; Kenneth E. Knight, "Changes in Computer Performance: A Historical View," *Datamation* (September 1966): 4–54; Robert J. Michael, "Hedonic Prices and the Structure of the Digital Computer Industry," *Journal of Industrial Economics* 27 (March 1979): 263–74; Brian T. Ratchford and Gerald Ford, "A Study of Prices and Market Shares in the Computer Mainframe Industry," *Journal of Business* 49 (April 1976): 194–218; idem, "Reply," ibid., 52 (1979): 125–34; Peter Stoneman, *Technological Diffusion and the Computer Revolution* (Cambridge: Cambridge University Press, 1976); and especially useful for summarizing the work of many, see Jack E. Triplett, "Price and Technological Change in a Capital Good: A Survey of Research on Computers," in Jorgenson and Landau, *Technology and Capital Formation,* 127–213.

58. For example, Knight, "Changes in Computer Performance"; see also Gregory C. Chow, "Technological Change and the Demand for Computers," *American Economic Review* 57 (December 1967): 117–30; Robert J. Gordon, "The Postwar Evolution of Computer Prices," in Jorgenson and Landau, *Technology and Capital Formation,* 77–125; Erich Bloch and Dom Galage, "Component Progress: Its Effect on High Speed Architecture and Machine Organization," *IEEE Computer* (April 1978): 64–75; Marie Anchordoguy, *Computers Inc.: Japan's Challenge to IBM* (Cambridge, Mass.: Council on East Asian Studies, Harvard University, 1989), passim.

59. Paul Stoneman, "Merger and Technological Progressiveness: The Case of the British Computer Industry," *Applied Economics* 10 (1978): 125–40.

60. Phister, *Data Processing Technology and Economics,* 329.

61. Ibid., 20.

62. Michael S. Mahoney, "The History of Computing in the History of Tech-

nology," *Annals of the History of Computing* 10, no. 2 (1988): 120.

63. The bulk of these can be studied in James W. Cortada, *Historical Dictionary of Data Processing: Organizations* (Westport, Conn.: Greenwood Press, 1987).

64. Ibid., 329.

65. Lavington, *Early British Computers,* 82–83.

66. Phister, *Data Processing Technology and Economics,* 32.

67. Ibid., 33.

68. Ibid.

69. J. Lear, "Can a Mechanical Brain Replace You?" *Colliers* 131 (April 4, 1953): 58–63. That mind set was evident elsewhere: P. Klass, "Giant Brains Could Aid Air Defense," *Aviation Week* 58 (May 11, 1953): 67–68; "Can Computing Machines Be Used by Businessmen to Formulate Major Decisions of Policy?" *Fortune* 48 (October 1953): 129; S. Fliegers, "Will Machines Replace the Human Brain?" *American Mercury* 76 (January 1953): 53–61; R. O. Kapp, "Do Electronic Brains Really Think?" *Science Digest* 33 (March 1953): 75–79.

70. Lear, "Can a Mechanical Brain Replace You?" 58–63.

71. Marshall Middleton, Jr., "Product Design by Digital Computers," *Westinghouse Engineer* (March 1956): 39–43.

72. E. Wainright Martin, Jr., *Electronic Data Processing: An Introduction* (Homewood, Ill.: Richard D. Irwin, 1961), 10.

73. Ibid., 32.

74. Ibid., 335.

75. Ibid., 58.

76. Ibid.

77. Ibid.; quote cited from "Office Automation Hits UAW," *Business Week* (April 9, 1960): 58.

Chapter 6

1. George Basalla, *The Evolution of Technology* (Cambridge: Cambridge University Press, 1988), 64–134.

2. James W. Cortada, *Before the Computer: IBM, NCR, Burroughs, and Remington Rand and the Industry They Created, 1865–1956* (Princeton, N.J.: Princeton University Press, 1993).

3. Frederick L. Fuller, *My Half Century as an Inventor* (n.p.: privately printed, 1938).

4. For bibliography on this theme see David A. Hounshell and John Kenly Smith, Jr., *Science and Corporate Strategy: DuPont R&D, 1902–1980* (Cambridge: Cambridge University Press, 1988), 731.

5. Most U.S. data centers continued to use 80-column card input and output into the early 1980s.

6. James Chposky and Ted Leonsis, *Blue Magic: The People, Power and Politics behind the IBM Personal Computer* (New York: Facts on File Publications, 1988); Paul Freiberger and Michael Swaine, *Fire in the Valley: The Making of the Personal Computer* (New York: Osborne/McGraw-Hill, 1984); Harold A. Layer, "Microcomputer History and Prehistory—An Archaeological Beginning," *Annals of the History of Computing* 11, no. 2 (1989): 127–30.

7. Alfred D. Chandler, Jr., *The Visible Hand: The Managerial Revolution in American Business* (Cambridge, Mass.: Harvard University Press, 1977), describes the process with various examples.

8. See Charles J. Bashe, Lyle R. Johnson, and John H. Palmer, *IBM's Early Computers* (Cambridge, Mass.: MIT Press, 1986), 167, for how sensitive the issue had become at IBM by the 1950s.

9. Isaac F. Marcosson, *Wherever Men Trade: The Romance of the Cash Register* (New York: Dodd, Mead, 1945): 92–108.

10. Franklin M. Fisher, James W. McKie, and Richard B. Mancke, *IBM and the U.S. Data Processing Industry: An Economic History* (New York: Praeger, 1983) 289–91, 399–401.

11. Cortada, *Before the Computer*.

12. These were the most sophisticated products tabulators in the 1920s and computers in the 1950s and, thus, could only be used by large organizations conducting large volumes of transactions that justified their cost.

13. James W. Cortada, *A Bibliographic Guide to the History of Computing, Computers, and the Information Processing Industry* (Westport, Conn.: Greenwood Press, 1990), lists hundreds of examples.

14. Many advertise in *ComputerWorld* and *Datamation,* two leading publications in the information-processing industry.

15. Lutze, "The Formation of the International Computer Industry, 1945–1960," 61.

16. Ibid., 141.

17. Dale W. Jorgenson, "Capital as a Factor of Production," in Dale W. Jorgenson and Ralph Landau, eds., *Technology and Capital Formation* (Cambridge, Mass: MIT Press, 1989), 1–35.

18. One of the best models is Marie Anchordoguy, *Computers Inc.: Japan's Challenge to IBM* (Cambridge, Mass.: Council on East Asian Studies, Harvard University, 1989); but see also Michael E. Porter, *The Competitive Advantage of Nations* (New York: Free Press, 1990).

Bibliographic Essay

This book is largely an exercise in defining the emergence of the computer as an example of how technology goes from laboratory to market. As a case study it did not require a detailed or definitive account of that story but identification of the main lines of development. I have told that story by relying largely on the works of the historians cited next. Comparisons with earlier office machines and identification of patterns of behavior found in the earlier office appliance industry came directly from research first presented in my book, *Before the Computer: IBM, NCR, Burroughs, and Remington Rand and the Industry They Created, 1865–1956* (Princeton, N.J.: Princeton University Press, 1993). Specific citations of sources are documented in the notes. The following titles will help those interested in exploring in more detail the issues raised in this book, particularly as they apply to the history of modern computing technology.

I have published a number of reference books designed to help students of the topic. *A Bibliographic Guide to the History of Computing, Computers, and the Information Processing Industry* (Westport, Conn.: Greenwood Press, 1990) offers more than forty-five hundred annotated references of which more than three thousand deal with the subject of this book. For an introduction to the major archival collections in the United States, see *Archives of Data Processing History: A Guide to Major U.S. Collections* (Westport, Conn.: Greenwood Press, 1990). It includes a detailed description of the Burroughs collection and those of other major firms in the industry from the 1880s forward. For an encyclopedic reference work see my three-volume *Historical Dictionary of Data Processing* (Westport, Conn.: Greenwood Press,

1987), which dedicates one volume each to technologies, biographies, and organizations and company histories.

For a history of the evolution of technology from ancient times to the present that puts accounting equipment and computers in perspective, see Michael R. Williams, *A History of Computing Technology* (Englewood Cliffs, N.J.: Prentice-Hall, 1985). In it he explains very clearly how machines worked. Along the same lines but with more of an application focus is a collection of articles edited by a distinguished computer science historian, William Aspray, *Computing before Computers* (Ames, Iowa: Iowa State University Press, 1990). The best technical history of early computers is by Paul E. Ceruzzi, *Reckoners: The Prehistory of the Digital Computer, from Relays to the Stored Program Concept, 1935–1945* (Westport, Conn.: Greenwood Press, 1983). Ceruzzi pays attention to many technical developments of early computing avoided by other authors.

The body of materials on the history of computers is now a growth industry in itself. My *Bibliographic Guide* lists hundreds of such titles. Particularly useful recent publications, however, include Nancy Stern, *From ENIAC to UNIVAC: An Appraisal of the Eckert-Mauchly Computers* (Bedford, Mass.: Digital Press, 1981); Kent C. Redmond and Thomas M. Smith, *Project Whirlwind* (Bedford, Mass.: Digital Press, 1980); William Aspray, *John Von Neumann and the Origins of Modern Computing* (Cambridge, Mass.: MIT Press, 1990); and Charles J. Bashe, Lyle R. Johnson, John H. Palmer, and Emerson W. Pugh, *IBM's Early Computers* (Cambridge, Mass.: MIT Press, 1986); these are definitive works on the early history of computers and their evolution from concepts to products.

Almost every history of the data-processing or computer industry provides some commentary on research and development of the computer from the 1930s forward. Of many such publications the most useful are Katharine Davis Fishman, *The Computer Establishment* (New York: Harper and Row, 1981), which is a general history; two books by a Brookings Institution economist, Kenneth Flamm, *Creating the Computer: Government, Industry, and High Technology* (Washington, D.C.: Brookings Institution, 1988), and *Targeting the Computer: Government Support and International Competition* (Washington, D.C.: Brookings Institution, 1987); and the well-illustrated history by Stan Augarten, *Bit by Bit: An Illustrated History of Computers* (New York: Ticknor and Fields, 1984).

A number of monographs fill in details on the early development of the computer: Herman H. Goldstine, *The Computer from Pascal to Von Neumann* (Princeton, N.J.: Princeton University Press, 1972), a technical history by a computer pioneer; Clark R. Mollenhoff, *Atanasoff: Forgotten Father of the Computer* (Ames, Iowa: Iowa State University Press, 1988); and Alice R. Burks and Arthur W. Burks, *The First Electronic Computer: The Atanasoff Story* (Ann Arbor: University of Michigan Press, 1988). A history intended for general audiences is Joel Shurkin, *Engines of the Mind: A History of the Computer* (New York: W. W. Norton, 1984). A more serious and effective treatment via a series of biographies is Robert Slater, *Portraits in Silicon* (Cambridge, Mass.: MIT Press, 1987). Two collections of papers on very early computing projects are Brian Randell, ed., *The Origins of Digital Computers: Selected Papers* (Berlin: Springer-Verlag, 1982), which is an anthology of important technical papers dating back into the nineteenth century, and N. Metropolis et al., eds., *A History of Computing in the Twentieth Century* (New York: Academic Press, 1980), consisting of papers by computer "pioneers" discussing their work of the 1930s and 1940s.

British computing is discussed in many of the publications already cited, but a useful brief history is Simon Lavington, *Early British Computers* (Bedford, Mass.: Digital Press, 1980), and the memoirs of a major British computer scientist, Maurice Wilkes, *Memoirs of a Computer Pioneer* (Cambridge, Mass.: MIT Press, 1985), which contains a great deal of material on U.S. developments in the 1940s and 1950s.

How companies responded to the computer can be gleaned from some company histories. Publications relative to specific companies described in this book vary in quality and quantity to such an extent that almost all firms of the period still await their historians. The best documented firm is IBM. A useful introduction to the company is by Robert Sobel, *IBM: Colossus in Transition* (New York: Times Books, 1981). A major memoir that offers considerable personal and professional information on IBM is by Thomas J. Watson, Jr., *Father Son & Co.: My Life at IBM and Beyond* (New York: Times Books, 1990). Another memoir useful for the period of the 1940s and 1950s is by William W. Simmons, *Inside IBM: The Watson Years* (Bryn Mawr, Pa.: Bantam, 1988). It is particularly useful for discussions on marketing at both field and corporate levels. Richly detailed for IBM and all early computer vendors is Franklin M. Fisher, James W. McKie, and

Richard B. Mancke, *IBM and the U.S. Data Processing Industry: An Economic History* (New York: Praeger, 1983). A beautifully illustrated history of NCR was published by the firm on its one hundredth anniversary in four booklets, *NCR: Celebrating the Future, 1884–1984* (Dayton, Ohio: National Cash Register, 1984). No company history of Burroughs covers the period of the computer, although the Burroughs Papers at the Charles Babbage Institute at the University of Minnesota are rich in detail. For Remington Rand there are only Stern's book on the UNIVAC and the memoirs of an early computer engineer there in the 1950s, Herman Lukoff, *From Dits to Bits: A Personal History of the Electronic Computer* (Portland, Ore.: Robotics Press, 1979).

For comparing the development of the computer to earlier information technologies, my *Before the Computer* is intended to be a detailed history of earlier devices and their industry. There are no histories of the cash register although many exist about the typewriter. The most useful are by M. H. Adler, *The Writing Machine—A History of the Typewriter* (London: George Allen and Unwin, 1973); W. A. Beeching, *Century of the Typewriter* (New York: St. Martin's Press, 1974); and the older Bruce Bliven, Jr., *The Wonderful Writing Machine* (New York: Random House, 1954). For a more economic view see George Nichols Engler, "The Typewriter Industry: The Impact of a Significant Technological Innovation" (Ph.D. diss., University of California at Los Angeles, 1969). An excellent biography of Herman Hollerith also describes the evolution of his punched-card technology, Geoffrey D. Austrian, *Herman Hollerith: Forgotten Giant of Information Processing* (New York: Columbia University Press, 1982). The only useful detailed look at calculating machines is by J. A. V. Turck, *Origin of Modern Calculating Machines* (Chicago: Western Society of Engineers, 1922). But see also books by Williams and Aspray about these machines that were cited previously.

Keeping up with the growing body of literature about computing's history and about its industry is an increasingly difficult task because the publication pace is picking up rapidly. The best aid is the *Annals of the History of Computing*, which lists new publications and carries book reviews and articles. The newsletter from the Charles Babbage Institute (the de facto archives of the information-processing industry) and the history newsletter of the IEEE provide useful current information on research, archival collections, and bibliography.

Several other studies have influenced the perspective of this book.

James R. Beniger, *The Control Revolution: Technological and Economic Origins of the Information Society* (Cambridge, Mass.: Harvard University Press, 1986), argued that information technology came into being in the post–Civil War period because it was really needed to help control the activities of large organizations. His book is particularly useful as an introduction to the discussion of the relationship of technology to American society for the period from the 1870s through the 1960s. Probably every historian of American business today has been influenced profoundly by the work of Alfred D. Chandler, Jr. A most useful book of his is *The Visible Hand: The Managerial Revolution in American Business* (Cambridge, Mass.: Harvard University Press, 1977), in which he shows the relationship of technology to the management of large organizations. David S. Landes provides a useful perspective on the effects of technology on an economy in his *The Unbound Prometheus: Technological Change and Industrial Development in Western Europe from 1750 to the Present* (Cambridge: Cambridge University Press, 1969).

George Basalla has examined how technology evolves over time, when it comes into existence, and why in *The Evolution of Technology* (Cambridge: Cambridge University Press, 1988). For an excellent study that describes the process whereby technological or science-based products move from laboratory to market, see David A. Hounshell and John Kenly Smith, Jr., *Science and Corporate Strategy: Du Pont R&D, 1902–1980* (Cambridge: Cambridge University Press, 1988). For a useful snapshot of the issues facing historians of technology in the early 1990s, see the proceedings of the *Conference on Critical Problems and Research Frontiers in History of Science and History of Technology,* October 30–November 3, 1991, Madison, Wisconsin (Madison: n.p., 1991).

Index

James W. Cortada holds a doctorate in history and has been with IBM for two decades in a variety of sales and management positions. Among his many books on the history and management of information technology are *Before the Computer* and the three-volume *Historical Dictionary of Data Processing*.